STORY OF
ENNEAGRAM

JULIETTE EDEN

Copyright © 2019 by Juliette Eden.

ISBN   Softcover   978-1-951469-83-2

All rights reserved. No part of this book may be reproduced or transmitted in any form or by any means, electronic or mechanical, including photocopying, recording, or by any information storage and retrieval system without express written permission from the author, except in the case of brief quotations embodied in critical reviews and certain other non-commercial uses permitted by copyright law.

Printed in the United States of America.

To order additional copies of this book, contact:
Bookwhip
1-855-339-3589
www.bookwhip.com

CONTENTS

Part One 7

    Section One 9
        Pentagram, Law of Existence 9
        Pentagram in Enneagramatic Scheme 13
        Triple Law of Existence 14

    Section Two 48
        Psychological Enneagrams with Pentagram Inside 48
        Picturing Enneagrams 65

Part Two 73

    Section One 75
        Individual Enneagrams 75

    Intermission 86

    Section Two 89
        Part One 89
        Part Two 94

    Section Three 106
        Enneagrams of Human Problematic 106

    Section Four 114

    Section Five 131

Part Three 137

    Section One 139
        Existential Enneagrams..139

    Section Two...152

    Section Three 168
        Modal Enneagrams..170
        Experiential Enneagrams 184
        Intermission 188

    Section Four 191

INTRODUCTION

When writing upon the subject, one puts oneself into concern. I am not responsible. You see it is difficult to put in words anything. A lot of philosophical accommodations just do not have place. I know, I cannot read. Whatever problems might arise for the reader, I might not be capable of sharing their situation. What is important is that it has been written and it is impossible to find any considerations for the book to be written or not, whatever prize, etc. There is no reason for writing, if you want. Any longer it does exist, like an atomic bomb, I cannot predict participation, annihilation, consequences, all kinds of treasure, carried out of the chamber. We know we are of concern. Who we are, what concern us, all this is completely indefinable. These questions are not posed, even if we need, we not right away recognize. One might consider not reading; it doesn't matter. You see, even no reader is no requirement. We know, we understand. The problem is then, how to survive it. One cannot go along. Any road is predictable, but this predictability is limited by our horizon. One cannot share other's opinion. We struck therefore upon the timeless question of any transmission at all, why would I do it? Let us suppose there is objectivity in terms of its factual, even this would not help us. As long as it is about letters, we are caught into the net of unpredictable necessity to keep our way, and we might never get out. So many people are never even coming to this realization; it is All Wrong. We read and we won't continue. You see, my problem is not in reproving or accommodating the reader to possible difficulties of the language, usage of words, possibly just hinting the meaning of the word completely different, which might be standing there as well, as in general, we are avoided; this is not difficult to predict even mis-consequences when one might think it was wrong usage, I don't know. What is of concern is that never before was I in order. I'm happy to do things how they should be done, but this is how I've been doing it. We know, we are looking for better, and one hits upon it, yes? The target, destination, we are not asked yet. I don't have to be better than everyone else. So many books I've just trashed down, literary and indirectly, disillusioned in my long-term love, as if I do not understand - it means I've grown up. Just old for this, it's how it happened. No, I just began to see something else; I didn't see this before. This is unknown, we don't understand; we think, and this is our thought. Why is it that what we reproduce makes this effect? I do not know. It means I am not qualified to write this book. Each and everyone is a misplaced person. We flow from the outward space toward an unclear goal, trying to define, and we don't understand, it is all black, with starry points around, maybe afar, not near. This introduction might not be necessary to put before the book on the Enneagram but I'm not sure what I wanted to bring into concern, by writing it. I touch very little upon questions sought now by politics, economy matters, popular stuff; this is not fiction. What is documentary? I don't even qualify for just reading it. And yet, there is nothing. It is difficult to see. I never dig out; I predisposed and predicted. One cannot be of concern. When you read, you don't notice this. This is why I warn.

PART ONE

Section One

Pentagram, Law of Existence

Traditionally, Enneagram begins in 9. Enneagram has nine points, and the circle is divided on nine parts, but there might be a greater number of stages. They might go behind the enneagramatic law. Placement of the *do* at point 9 is correct, but it is not necessarily a top point. In practice, the design of Enneagram is made after the period, emerging at the division of figures from one to seven on 7. This period is changing its numbers in sequence:

1/7=0.142857
2/7=0.2857142

Figures 3, 6, and 9 are absent in the period, as well as zero. Next, he says 7/7=0.99999. It is correct like a theory, still 7/7=1 and this is not quite explained. G. Gurdjieff says figure nine is connected with six and three, all of them not included in a period. This gives the inner triangle of Enneagram. 8/7=1.142857 that is the division of sequential after seven numbers gives new cycle of period, where first begins from 0 and second from 1. It might go till 13 where it will be 1.857142 till completion of cycle where 14 divided to 7 produces 2. If we are serious about digital order and believe it to be an indication to discovery of attributes of creation and created, it is as well an enneagramatic scheme, only with another position.

Figures 3, 6, and 9, not entering into period could be connected into triangle. The main is that figure made by the line of a period is symmetrical to triangle 9-3-6. Digits of period go around the circle. 0 is a symbol of circle; it is an enclosed cycle. Gurdjieff says 7/7=0.9 and places nine into an apex of Enneagram. If 7/7=1 then it is 10, as figure 1 stands *before* the point, on the order higher, and top point of Enneagram is 10, with numbers seven and four at the corners of the base of the triangle with intervals placed symmetrically.

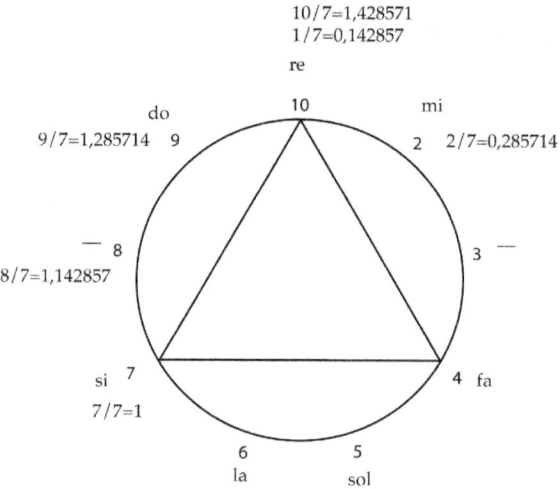

Figure one is absent, but it is assumed. Circle is an enclosed cycle. Figure zero is a symbol of enclosure. There are ten ones at point ten, or [1xcycle]. Division of 10 to 7 will give sequential period: 1.42857...

Ten is the beginning. Beginning cannot be a result. Triangle 10-7-4 is a source, law of octave, and law of three. Three forces invariably evoke the fourth: active+neutral+passive=result. This is not triplicity. Triplicity is exemplified by the number 3, or a result, taken in its three components. These three phenomena give rise to the existence. Intervals are places of slowing. Enneagram traditionally has the process going around the circle with numbers included in the period connected in between by the line; this connection corresponds to the inner sequence. This periodic line is a mechanical law. Period works only for functional phenomenon. If to take as an example few functional enneagrams, it is easy for us to place the stages, considering points of the change in the process. In manufacturing of cloth, first, dress is designed, then it has to be cut out of fabric and sewn, and appear in the store; it might then be chosen by the public. In functional enneagrams, there are ten stages, one initial and a result. Process of manufacture is completely functional, and here stages are mirrored:

Customer — Designer
Choosing the fabric and style — Choosing the dress fashioned so and so.

Here, the intentional line is very clear. When a designer designs the dress, he is considering the customer. Cutting out a pattern is done with the use of a model, offered by the designer, and they don't change anything. At the final stage of completion, they consider how the product is going to look in a shop to be chosen. When choosing the dress, we think of the designer. The customer thinks of how this dress is going to look upon him, if it is of good quality, and would he feel comfortable in it. Finally, we have dressed up a man. The process was set up by a requirement to be dressed, so that a designer had to produce the pattern.

Enneagram of Manufacture of Cloth

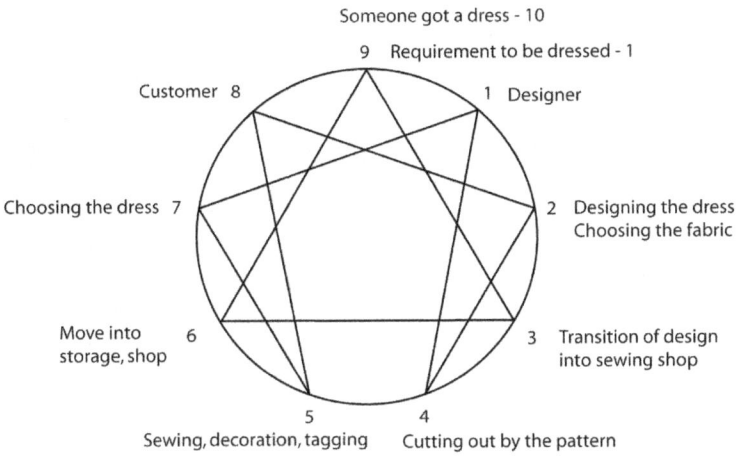

If to compare manufacture with planting, it will be a bit different, because here it is something about natural process.

Enneagram of Growing Plants

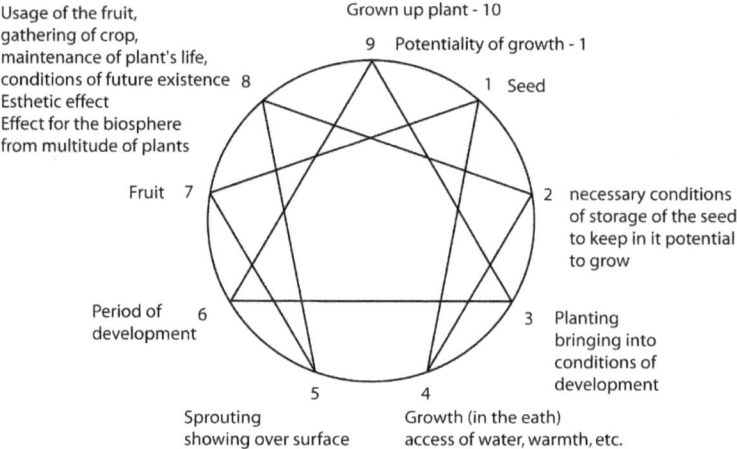

Nine is a whole totality of natural process, kept by the main. Two is a situational problem. Three is entry of the new octave, four is development, five is result and novelty, and six is the move into hidden (or open.) Seven is production, it should be consistent or it fails.

Ten, seven, and four produce the possible world. Four is a result of three forces. 1+2+3=6. It is six other points of enneagram together with three initial forces. Seven is an octave with two intervals giving nine points of enneagramatic scheme. Entry (3), newness (5), transition (6), and exemplification (8) enter with source (10) into existential pentagram. What is left is development (4), production (7) — the top corner of triangle being 10; and whole (9) and situation (2).

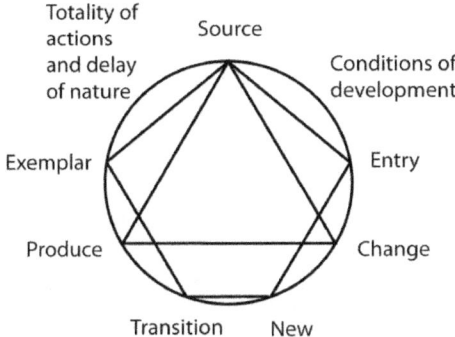

Point three is a place of moving in another direction. Four is a stage of change of condition. A new emerges; it is the fifth stage. Six is transition; if at point six another shock doesn't come (some influence upon this particular process) then it "transits" into another direction, not to the "fruit" of the work. If the process is influenced well, we receive the fruit at the seventh stage. Then we have to gather and clear after the job (8). We might need to review and this leads to certain actions, which would constitute another enneagram, because every stage might be viewed as a single enneagram with its nine correlative phenomena. Then either the whole process is "reborn" and starts again or if it continues but not in the same set, there will be another enneagram. (New tree, giving fruits every season, or new seed to be planted.)

Pentagram in Enneagramatic Scheme

10.7.4	Triangle of source, octave, and result
10.8.6.5.3	Pentagram
2 and 9	Places of slowing

Triple Law of Existence

Places of slowing together with the source enter into the law of existence

1. Situation, slowing, conditions of development
2. Triplicity, entry
3. Law of four elements, change
4. Joy, happiness, novelty
5. Rule, order, transition
6. Octave, fruit
7. Exemplar, correction
8. Whole
9. Source, beginning, labor, truth

Five appear from three.

FIVE ELEMENTS

                        Source

Correction   Triplicity

                Rule   Joy
           Legislation   Happiness

Five appear from three.

Ratio of division of nine on ten points of circumference

2	4.5	
3	3	
4	2.25	Conditions of development
5	1.8	
6	1.5	
7	1.285714285714	
8	1.125	
9	1	Whole
10	0.9	

How from triangle 10, 7, and 4 to receive 8, 3, 6, and 5

10+4=14 (1+4=5)

10+7=17 (1+7=8)

10−4=6

10−7=3

Source + law of seven (octave) = correction

Source + rule (law of three) = joy and happiness

Source − rule (law of three) = law, legislation (order)

Source − law of seven (octave) = triplicity

Juliette Eden

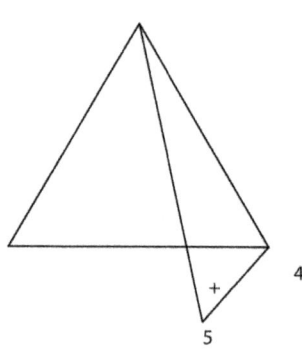

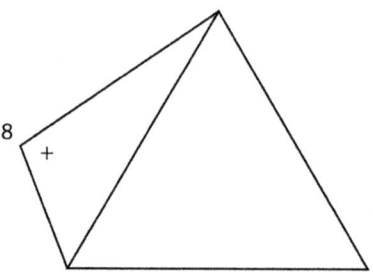

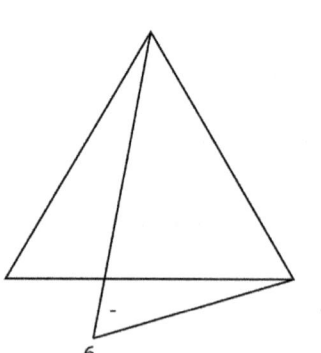

Story of Enneagram

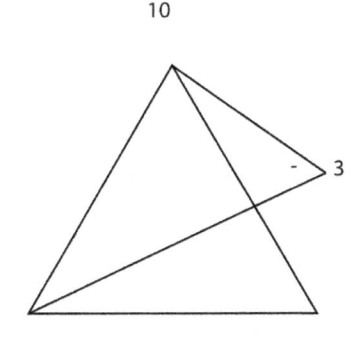

Correction
Triplicity
Joy
Order

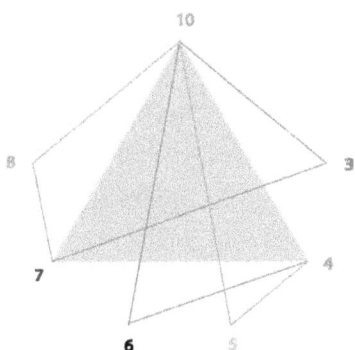

Common Figure

Green lines designate negative trans-connections; orange designate positives.
4, 6, 10, 3, 7, 8, 10, 5, 4 – LINE OF EXISTENCE

Four could be seen also as a law; law of four in existential totality of phenomenon. Then six, to distinguish it from four, is a grief because it is an ordering; it is absence of joy because joy is an exceptionally high point, desirable to be reached, and if it is conditioned so that there is no exit out of the line, then man feels vacancy of such existence. In this way, existence, if for the aim of its only existence in "order," is a grief; life is irregular initially and happiness is a consequence of coming together of different factors. It cannot be produced and distributed equally between people. In abstract form, joy is necessary when one is separated and "differs."

Law, grief, beginning, triplicity, octave, improvement, beginning, joy, law…

From law to grief to beginning, from beginning to triplicity and octave, from seven to improvement and beginning, from there to joy and back to law.

This line is not a period. The sequence works only for processes or phenomena/events when something is created, and where there is a pentagram. This is very close, because what we think already has been created; some phenomenon might be still in creation. It might seem odd the necessity to move through one and the same stage of beginning, but it might have a particular sense, which has to be sought out in practice, as well as enclosure—repetition of starting point—the four, for completion. It might also be that if it is a line, it should be applicable to the existential process, and if it is phenomenon in its creation, it is about a link in between three initial forces and four more stages that arouse out of them.

Fact of there being on one stage of enneagram a place of negative factor means that in any process, even positive, there is going to be a dark side in it. Depending upon is it a phenomenon, factual process, abstraction, this would have different approaches in the enneagramatic scheme. Sometimes it is just a crucial point. Sometimes it is just a transition.

Because position of the numbers is exchanged, a periodic line 1-4-2-8-5-7 would be placed aslant. In such an enneagram, with triangle 10-4-7, if there is a period it means there is a functional process in it. The periodic line is put at an angle because it is existential enneagram, but it has functional process in it as well.

If we would take as an example creation of world, it is a descending enneagram, because it runs from the source into manifestation, so that it is 10, 9, 8, etc. It is very good example to show that descending enneagram process goes simultaneously both ways. It is creation of substance from minuscule parts (10). The beginning, or source, at the same time it is a basic molecule of substance, which is used for arousal of everything. Then it is a whole of whatever there are (9), and slowing and situation of factors (2). Correction and planning (8) corresponds to triplicity of natural arising (3). Then there are problems of tension, because existence, if the aim isn't reached yet, presupposes it. In a way it is octave, which has to be straightened and work for corresponding shocks (7). From another side it is legality, four elements of any natural event we accept this and we don't work for it, it is phenomenal. Then it is law and word, bondage and freedom.

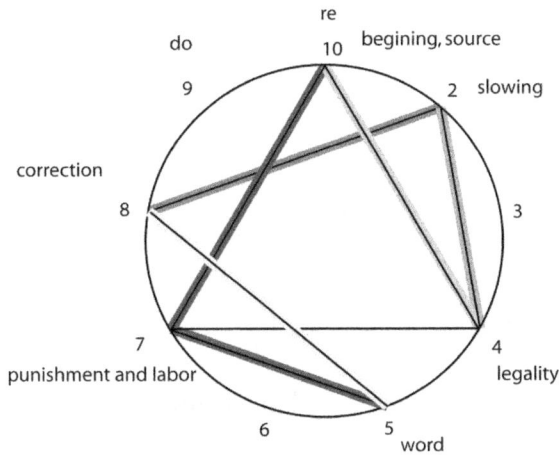

Enneagram with the Law of Move

Rose line from beginning to law of three is the creation of a material world. Pale violet line from law to slowing down, passing through triplicity is development of organic matter. Green line from slowing to correction, past beginning and struggle, is emerging of sensation. From eight to five, or correction and word, goes the lightest line with yellow hue. From word to punishment and labor through the grief goes the black line of inward development. From seven back to the source, through the correction and struggle, man returns to God.

10 – 4	material world
4 – 2	organics
2 – 8	sensitivity
8 – 5	word, mentation
5 – 7	inward possibility of growth
7 – 1	development

If to look at the pentagram, beginning and higher influences in accord with the world's phenomena open up the possibility of realization and as a consequence, happiness, when without this phenomenal feature, it brings up an ordering. If we work upon the octave by means of higher truth, etc., then we have a correction; we need to have shocks for an octave to be straight. Both "additions" are a step higher on enneagramatic scheme, Joy, 5 after four, and Correction, 8 after seven. Stages appearing by deduction stand a step lower, but they are swapped.

Universal Enneagram, basic scheme

Light upon the earth is not only light from upward; it is light of any particular concentration.

Story of Enneagram

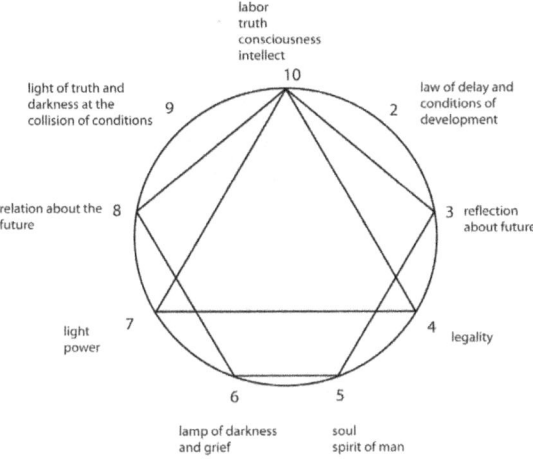

Enneagram of Light

10	labor, truth, consciousness, intellect
9	light of truth and darkness at collision of conditions
8	relation about the future
7	light, power
6	lamp of darkness and grief
5	soul, spirit of man
4	legality
3	reflection about the future
2	law of delay and conditions of development

In a human being, truth is a soul, or spirit, if there is no soul. A situation also can be clarified with its problematic and barriers preventing of realization of whatever aim we might have. There is light and power, as there is light and power in general. Light of anima is its naturalness, it is brought to existence by the law, and it continues to be animated by the law, so it is legal. We might be predisposed to have an intuitive approach toward future moments of our life. It is not done by us in actuality, but this "look out of truthful part of reality" might move us toward refusal of what might surf us. The world won't be complete if no ability would exist of approaching the stage permitting a direct knowledge. This is the difference in between reflection and relation about the future. Instead of just a situational problem, we might have a war of opposing factors inside us; if it is about light, this conflict is brought as by impossibility outwardly to carry on our decision, based upon wish (so that it's important) but by the inner struggle of our own negative factor, which might enter and work for the situation with its pressure, so that we have to encounter it at this condition. There is a separation in between good and bad, and there has to be such a separation, so that there is as a spiritual lighter, but sorrow as well. It gives us a neutral triangle of higher light, which might be accepted as all holy ever present one, and just legality and power; light at the clarification of outward and inward collision of conditions; approaches of illuminating the procedure to make a choice, and two separated situations when it is reached and concentrated, or it is reversed.

Enneagram of Luck

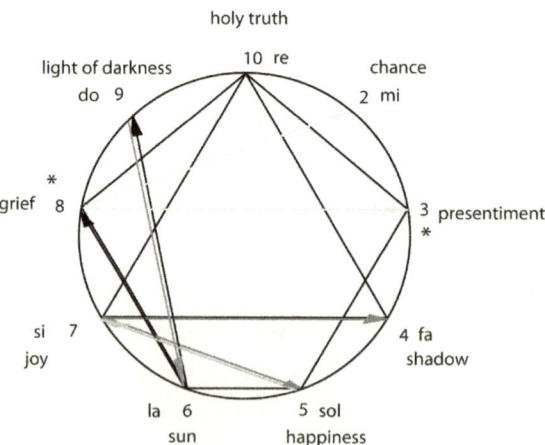

Arrangement of world

Joy is the inward feeling of goodness and light (luminosity)

Shadow—light from the sun, darkening of reason, visible world.

Light of darkness—sun shines everywhere, there is also another lighter.

We predict...what? What will be there?

Truth—the best link in the chain of events.

Truth
Joy
Shadow

Chance
Happiness
Grief

Light of Darkness
Sun
Presentiment

10
2
3
4
5 → 7
6 → 8, 9
7 → 4, 5
8 → 2, 3
9 → 6

7 8 9 5 4 3 2 6

The row of sequence

Shadow and sun
Grief and joy
Light of darkness and truth
Chance and Happiness

Predicament

Chance is a turn in events. The predicament is important in terms of presence or absence of luck. It is in a way a stage, around which it is going on. If there won't be a misfortune, significance of luck would be null. Other stages fall into four pairs of two opposite factors. In each of the three triangles there is a main factor and two opposing factors:

Truth Joy   Chance Happiness Presentiment Sun
       Shadow Grief   Light of darkness

The meaning of one of the elements is backed up by two secondary ones. Chance might bring happiness or grief; or, we are happy at feeling truth, or are shadowed, not having it.

Arrows indicate the exchange in qualities in between factors.

Enneagram of Caress

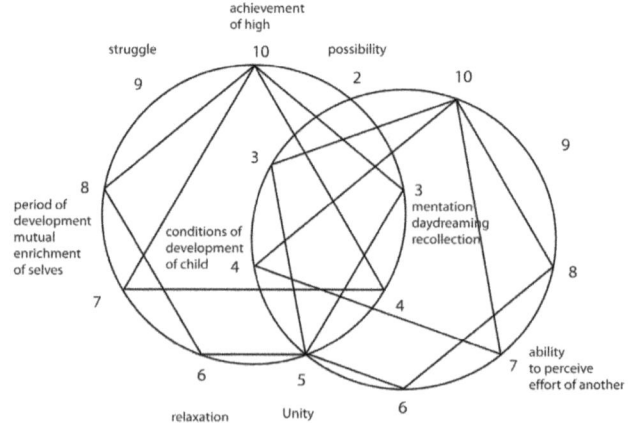

2 – conditions of development – possibility
3 – dreams, memories
4 – conditions of development of child
5 – happiness, joy – unity
6 – relaxation
7 – ability to perceive effort of another
8 – mutual enrichment of selves, period of development (future)
9 – struggle
10 – achievement of high

Not a flat surface, it is seen from the back.

Enneagrams might intersect at one and the same stages. In the diagram it is shown as one of it being reversed. It is not so; diagrams are arranged so as all stages of both enneagrams would be seen in flat. For both partners the process here is one and the same, but we can see that the coincidence happens at situational possibility and unity of intercourse, even if we can imagine both enneagrams sequentially passing through all of the stages coming to them simultaneously. It might be that they traverse each other's circumference, but still this process is about coming together for unification, and this might happen only if there is a possibility — all other stages might have happened without a real intercourse. Even if there is an intercourse without unity, then it is not enneagram of caress; it is some another situation. All feelings we might have, and abilities, enter into this enneagram.

Even the simplest process might be put in nine steps. For example, fall of a raindrop. The triangle consists from water's structure, world arrangement, and floating at the sky. With the structure water has, with this world arrangement, it might float upward in its gaseous state. Then we have conditions of fall and joy of fall. To fall, there should be a necessary amount of it; it is a preliminary (successful gathering at sky.) When it falls it dissolves. And then it may again return to the sky.

Fall of Raindrop

Structure of water
Conditions of fall
Successful gathering at the sky
World arrangement
Joy of fall
Dissolution and decay
Floating at the sky
Calculation and knowledge of the main
Return to the sky

When we speak of time, we consider our human situation. It is often about the position of arrows upon the watch. But Time's very nature is undefined. We should accept it as a given that there is an unconditional time from the capital letter. But it is not enough for its manifestation; for time's entry exists its substitute, which plays a part in processes and events. This enters at fourth stage, as a world's requirement. There is also intention, as a flow of time. As physical factors, there is a point and a period. There should be. Then it is the ability to perceive time and what we perceive as a transition. It disappears. Then it is spread and calculation. If there is planning, we might as well calculate the periods in terms of its transition. (9-6-3)

Transition is the barrier, processing of qualities, deviation, decay, passing away…

Calculation
Barrier, transition
Period

Glan is ability to feel the time, condition of counting

Enneagram of Time

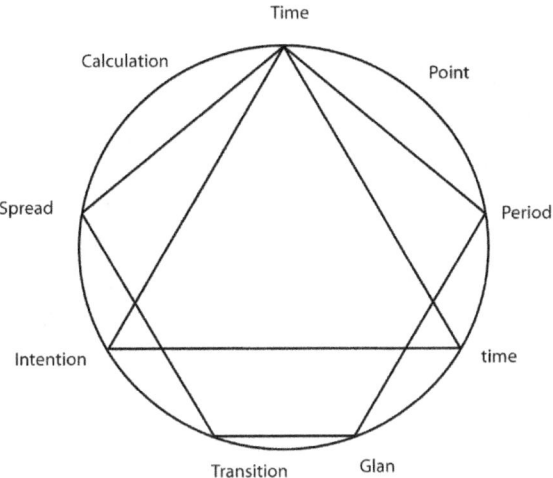

Second Enneagram of Caress

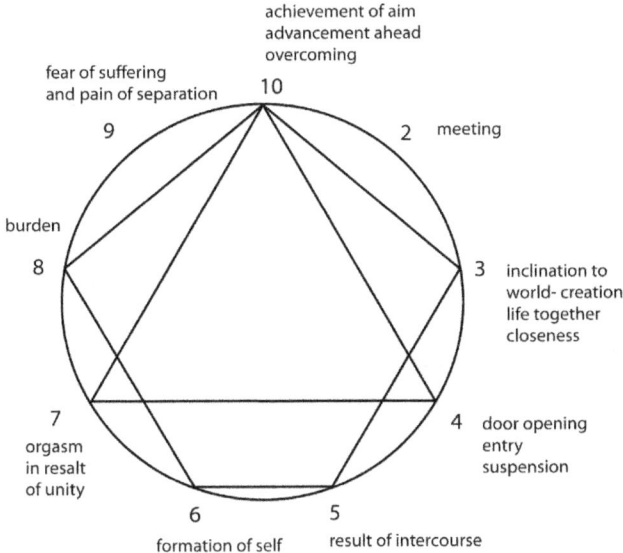

In terms of intercourse, there are particular stages that we did not mention. It is easy to realize particular factors if to view it as an act, its consequences, and our reaction. 10-7-4 is three powers entering into an activity. The situational triangle includes the meeting, result of the intercourse itself, and the possible reality of carrying a child. Three is the creative factor in our reactions, 6 is negation, because it negates the intercourse. We might not think of someone wishing to see us, meet us again. Suffering and not desiring to be separated is a requirement for continuation. Arrows might help to understand the exchange and connection in between factors. Five is a joy, so 5→7 is a higher point over enneagram. Arrows lead from seven to four and five; it is the relationship. From eight to 2 and 3, it is the situational part. The heaviest part falls at nine and eight, as a burden and pain being separated, or fear of it or possible miscarriage.

Perception by Visual Means

For abstract representation of things in space with their outlines and shades, we need a device. This brings up an existence of a material object, the eye. Then it depends upon where we are, what the conditions are at looking, how healthy is an eye. The ability to assimilate is a crucial part. Out of what we have perceived, by means of knowledge, out of this accepted information we receive the shock to act. In acting, we touch back upon abstract representation, only of another enneagram.

8 – correction → an eye, ray
7 – law of octaves → mechanics, eyesight
6 – grief → main and light
9 – position of conditions at collision of efforts → knowledge
5 – happiness → task

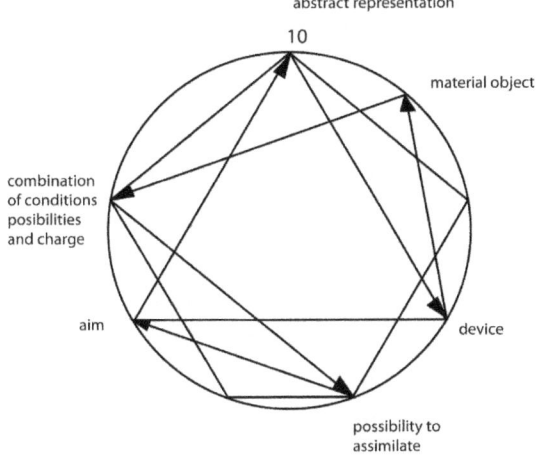

An eye – apparatus for perception
Eyesight – ability to perceive
Mechanics – device
Light – conditions of perception at which one can see
Knowledge – possibility to assimilate
Task – aim appearing in result of processing of coming data
Main is position of conditions, possibilities, and charge
Ray – condition of existence of efforts
Representation – abstract perception of effort

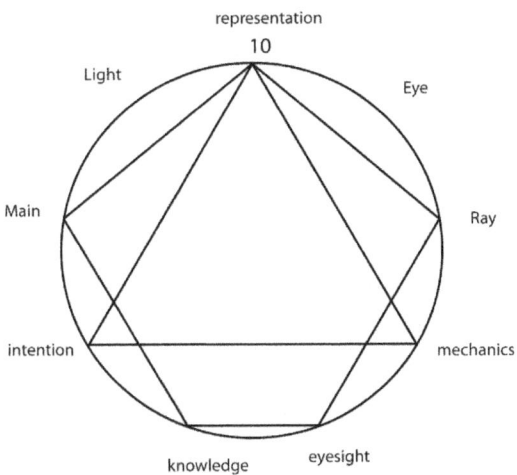

Task appears from the ability to assimilate.

This is the enneagram of ignorance. It has two parts. The enneagram is a symbol, but here it is in a scheme, and we can picture some stages of two processes to intercede. I make them intercede at 10 of both enneagrams and 4 of one with 7 of another. The idea of having two enneagrams for one and the same thing is that one of it is abstract and the second is functional. Having an aim leads to cognition, or intentionality brings up to it, then language takes it upon itself to «fix» the meaning. Our language evokes in us tenderness or inclination to the usage of certain vocabulary acting. Then we have an obstacle—not everything could be said, there might be things we are not acquainted with, therefore we cannot express them by our language, which we use, and using it we cut ourselves from what is not out of what we usually give definition to. This is functional enneagram.

Enneagram of Ignorance

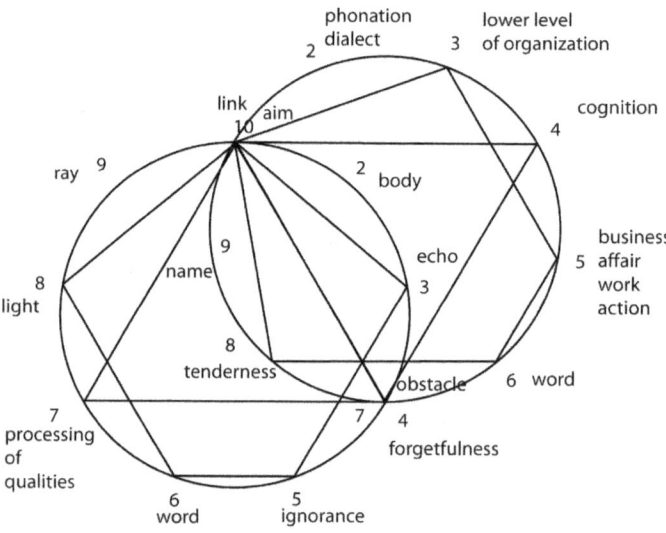

Link   Aim
Ray   Name

Light	Tenderness
Processing of qualities	Obstacle
Word	Word
Ignorance	Business
Forgetfulness	Cognition
Echo	Lower level of organization
Body	Phonation, dialect

Data is linked in between its parts; if we forget, processing of qualities goes wrong. Echo is a reverberation or reaction in people, of the word. Ray is indication. Light is clarification. We forget connection in between data, speaking about the real facts (for example.) Then we hear the word; we have a reaction and indication of explanation. Then we "explain" in our ignorance all of what isn't clear. There is interconnection in between abstract intellectual cognition and mechanism of using sentences for expression. With the aim we link data together, but we have forgotten we connect it with our disability of expression, so that whole of functional enneagram has its result (7) when abstract one has its cause. This way, abstract enneagram is independent and reflexive is brought to the beginning without realization of deceptive nature of its mechanics.

Enneagram of the Flow of Business

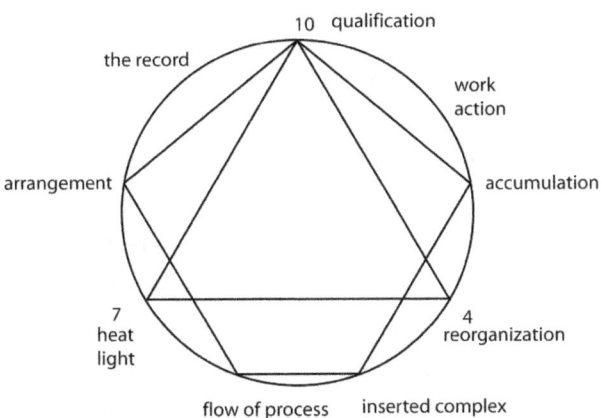

Flow of business is put into job by a power (7). To ensure its good work, reorganization, or its possibility is required, as well as it should qualify for possible transactions. Functional triangle 2-5-8 is work, shelving things and entry, and the setting. Accumulation, record, and flow of process relate to the flow of process itself, to its nature.

Enneagram of Identity of Theme

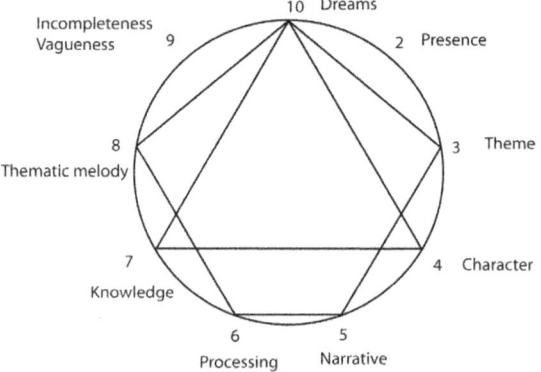

Presence	Incompleteness
Theme	Thematic melody
Quality Info,	content
Narration	The process

Imagination

We recognize the theme by certain qualities, which are put into enneagram. It is imaginary control of thematic development (8 and 3) along with the narrative and processing—it is pentagram. Character as a signature and informative content is an underground; if it is not put in accord with the theme, the product is destroyed. If the character and content do not correspond to the theme, it cannot be recognized. Dreams put into character make up the work with narration and its procedure. Content makes up for the theme. In any theme there is a presence, but there is also a place for incompleteness.

Enneagram of Universe

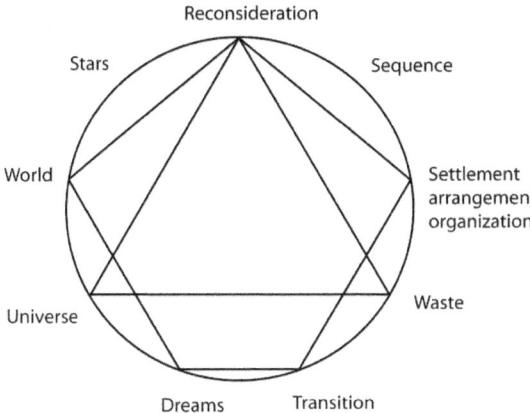

The enneagram of universal matter separates on three parts of actual, plan, and dissolution.

Universe	World	Stars
Reconsideration	Sequence	Settlement
Waste	Transition	Dreams

So, it is the universe made up by galaxies, which consist of stars.

Enneagram of All Knowledge

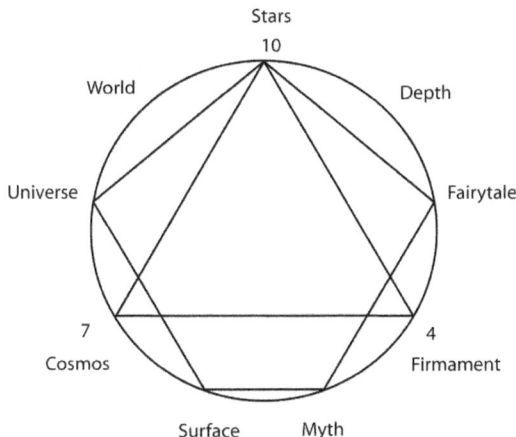

Every transition evolves another kind of mental acceptance of all knowledge from horizon with special qualities.

Depth	perception of things with deeper, but clear meaning
Firmament	stiff or very traditional; put by society opinions
Surface	banal opinions without any ground
Myth	an expression of here being more than it is actually told, expectation
Fairytale	remnants of former cultural accumulation, perversion
Stars	scientific acts
Cosmos	a spatial accordance of oneself and substance of answer, penetration
World	a natural sciences, biology
Universe	a view of processes in their true nature

Creation of Anything

Problem is concretization of things, abstraction is the thinkable in general, and song is its spontaneous resolving. The only possible argumentation toward decisions gives a result at the set of possible conditions. There is responsibility as well as misleading in the act of every creation, but it aspires to the concretization, or it's nothing. If there is a creation there is a result. It involves problematic of creation. We need to balance in between our responsibility about the result, and a certain amount of freedom. This is the functional half of enneagram. Song, or spontaneous decision, proceeds by integration of abstraction with concrete factors, using a theorem, or the only argument, at the situation (conditions), which is given as a stage at which a result should proceed. These four, except song, are an abstraction.

Enneagram of Creation

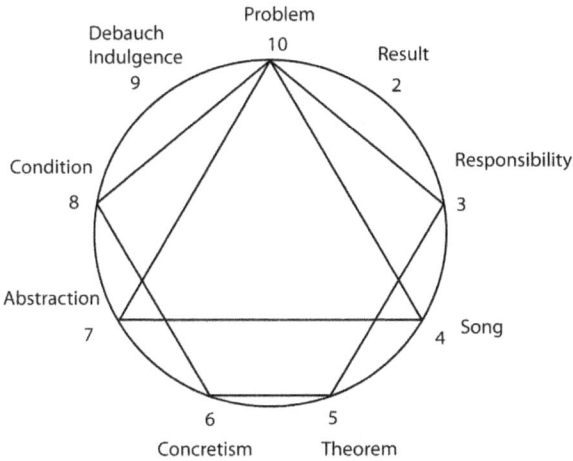

Enneagram of Reflections

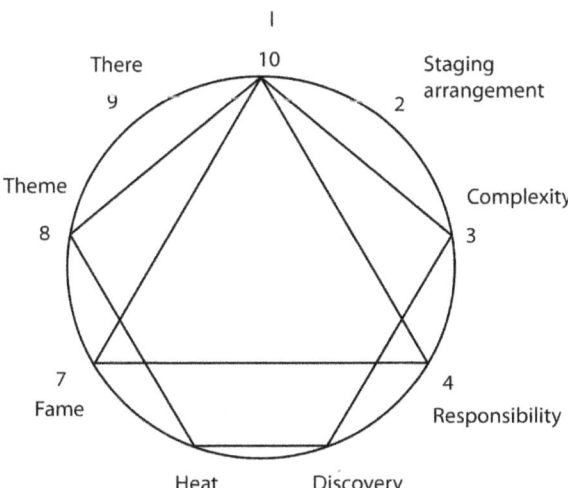

For the soul concentration there is a set of arranging conditions. There is indication (9.) The more we do the more complex a route toward arousal of necessary factors is. Discovery leads to fame. For good concentration, we need heat, or sweat; only responsibility cannot accomplish the job. We might have our theme for this.

Juliette Eden

I
There   } individual
Theme
Fame
Heat   } situation, arrangement
Discovery
Responsibility
Complexity   } conditions, setting
Staging, arrangement

We might have reflection in themselves of what is outside, it is akin of to interpret or accept and put in order subjects that we have deciphered.

10 → 4   self-control
4 → 2   operating in a field
2 → 8   the leading idea, search of better materialization
8 → 5   realization
5 → 7   spread around of final product

Direction (9)   Efforts (6)   Structure (3)

Direction	Staging	*spatial*	outward situation
Theme	Structure	*embodiment*	what we work upon
Fame	Responsibility	*human factor*	inward aspiration
Efforts	Discovery	*actualization*	production

I, the subject and production, make a pentagram, enclosed in outward and inward factors.

Story of Enneagram

Enneagram of Bravery

Bravery is a quality permitting us to manifest toward destruction of undesired features, without consideration of personal loss, for the fact that the loss would be bigger and is accepted as such at the permission of these undesired factors to enter. In this idea is also included the opening itself, as well as conditions or data of personal factual concentration (4, 3, 2). Bitterness is manifestation even if with the true reasonable considerations, but done under the surveillance of deep feeling of offence and personal inadequacy. This includes the idea of possibly existing powers, in resources, or ever-present, and reaction (cruelty). Our opinion of others has nothing to do with their real person, but still it enters into the process of reorganization: do they deserve it, or not, so… There is longing and struggle to come out to the place where we would conserve features in order to preserve our own I. Freedom and invulnerability of a personal matter is the result of our courage to insinuate the process of coming into the open with its possible dangers.

From human opinion, bravery is an action of being brave at the circumstances that demand it. In a way, we can substitute any action of bravery and apply it to the scheme. The enneagram tells us that courage isn't a result of coming factors; it has its beginning as a preexistent trait.

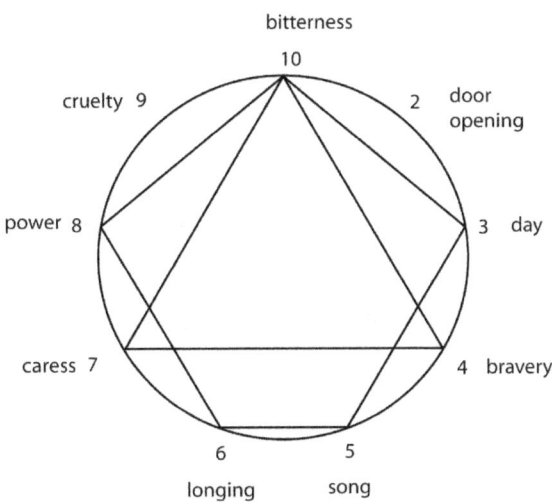

Inclinatory Triplet

2	entry into open
5	freedom of behavior
8	capability to destroy for good

Struggle of an I

3	a special concentration or matter of particular «flour» feeling
6	reaching or wish of actuality
9	a pressure of social factors

Collision of Human Factors

4	bravery, a special quality of destruction of opposite, by means of personal
7	tenderness, love toward humanity as universal so and personified
10	displeasure, sour factor, instability, to manifest truly but out of offence

Bravery	beginning
Day	condition (human of body qualification)
Door	opening entry, classification and reactionary factor, exchange
Bitterness	sour feeling of loss and fall, offended by…
Cruelty	appearing out of preceding stage resultant feature
Power	power to remove it
Caress	recognition of love
Longing	desire to come out
Song	song of resurrection

Example of "substituted" (in this case) applied factor (particular) on the usage of *bravery*.

Enneagram of Elevation

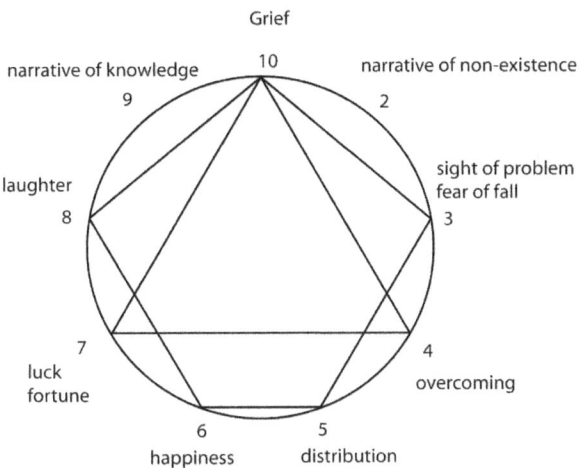

Grievance is a feature of instability. To rise high, we need to overcome it. It happens with the luck. Non-existential character of any concentration is ever present at the moments or positions where no self-control is present. Laughter means attitude that "nothing matters", which prevents us to realize what solution could be found for situation, and to see pattern of our reactions and how it affects our misconception about what have happened or would happen later. To distribute all possible factors, there is this stage (5). But this distribution happens whether we want it to or not and this is why it is in [negative] triad. Sight of problem and fear of fall is a feature of conscious participation in action of life overcome, but it gives theory of possible danger at every elevation. Happy to be, but it also has another side of being happy for no reason, or when there is a danger behind, it's usual. It is negation. A long story of what has happened at life's situation before and clear cognition at least partially of true nature of facts makes up a ninth stage.

Juliette Eden

Luck, fortune	sweetness of being forever in favor
Happiness	a special character or featuring point
Distribution	the possible low-birth of behavior
Overcoming	an opposing factor toward anything
Sight of problem, fear of fall	the predicament of misfortune
Narrative of nonexistence	absence of mind
Grief	final misunderstanding of position
Narrative of knowledge	what has happened was an accident
Laughter	whatever, it's wrong to come with an issue

Substitute for "non-elevation" (with its possibility) event

Theorem of Nonexistence

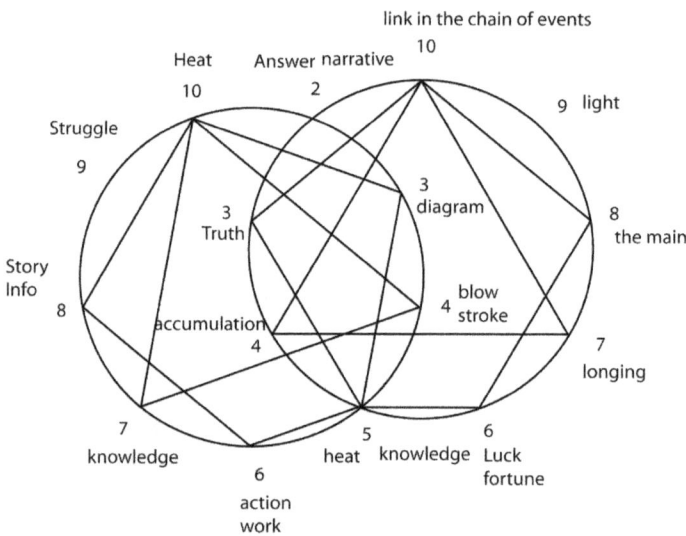

Heat	link in the chain of events
Struggle	light
Story, info	main
Knowledge	longing

Action, work	luck, fortune
Heat	knowledge
Blow, stroke	accumulation
Diagram	truth
Answer	narrative

This is the theorem of nonexistence, consisting of two parts — mental and energetic. Schematic diagrams traverse over the second and fifth stages of each other; we can see the mental diagram in reverse for better observation of interconnection in between both processes. Light and truth with fortune constitute a triad of possible development. In energetic enneagram it is a struggle; efforts toward the ... by means of a planning. Link in the chain of events is an impossible constitution of self-cognition through sequence of events; phenomenal world brings upon a longing. Accumulation is a requirement. 2, 5, and 8 is a mentality. 10 (Heat) is energy, 5 (heat) is fuel. Please look at the end of the book for *what this scheme is about.*

Enneagram of Answer

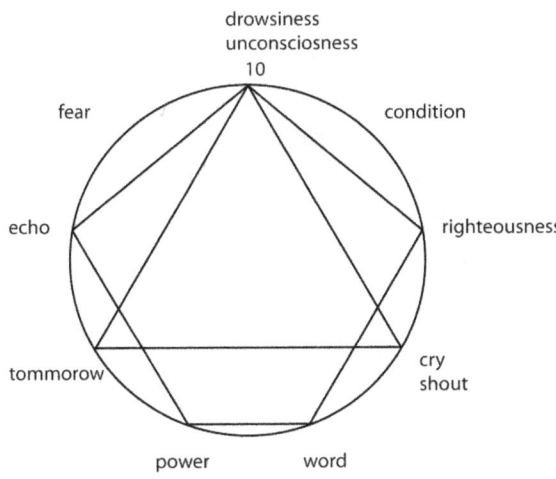

Enneagram of answer consists from an impossible condition in which we cannot do anything, scale of values in terms of what should be right. Answer, response of inward self to outside, like manifestation. Letter of freedom; instability of powers, future act of reincarnation at «another day»; vibrations outward into atmosphere. Fear of continuation. Our inner state of irregular «awakening» to the situation. [from 2 to 10]

Period of transition	instability of facts, waiting period
Sweetness of arms	approach, recognition
Cross of bearing oneself	feeling of blame
Fear of not being recognized	loneliness
Lips of wonder	naiveté
Caress of slip	the fall (as moral tells, maybe true)
Come toward, I'm flying	elevation, momentary, periodic
Let's do it	pressure
Hold stronger, I'm yours	resurrection of beloved' linkage

Enneagram of Continuation of Undesired Link

Capture is a state from which we cannot make a free decision. It is characterized by acts of power, possibly intelligent and with intention, which go toward the person under fire. Disposition of events is for situation. → Man who we are dealing with (human factor) → Who exactly is it? → Self-problematic, our inner awareness of being closer to the fire. → Loss of possibility to manifest in desired direction and failure of controllability. → Deciphering of situational outcome and points of transaction. → Failure of any possible decision or acts of immediate rescue. → The disposition of immediate factors → all gathered knowledge → Anew

Enneagram of capture

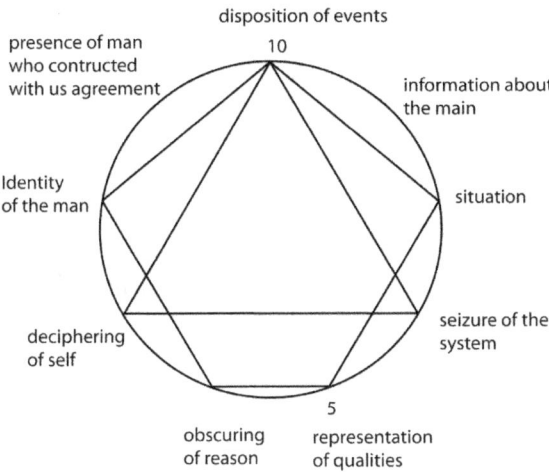

A period

Stage, situation, circumstances

 *Approach*

Loss, subject to action of power, inadequacy at this situation

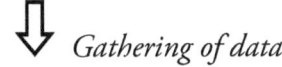 *Gathering of data*

Considered important info of all the features leading or suppressing us

⇩ *Looking up at the problem (because it is pressure by one man)*

Who is, what is the mask of the person, his intentions

⇩ *Move into inner resources of judgment (for function)*
Spread of qualities of whatever we have under examination (self)

Qualification of all the features of power force, situation, toward pressure acting

 Transiting to a man at the wheel—ourselves (personality) Realization of self-inadequacy and not being able to get out (real)

Self-examination, experience of being disposed

 Getting back to power-leading (actuality and obscuring) Retrieval

Back to disposition of affairs

Enneagram of Transition of the Air

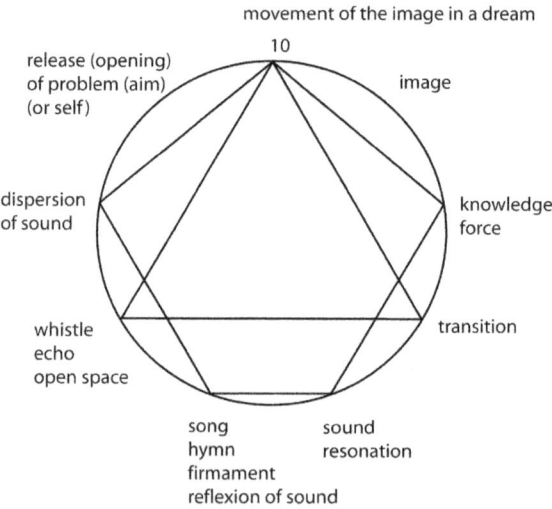

movement of the image in a dream	our representation of non-existential
whistle, echo, open space	perspective, horizon, where could it come from?
transition	now we see it, now we don't

image	caress at the bar, non-spatial action, light air's touch
dispersion of sound	possibility of transition
sound, resonation	response
force, knowledge	forceful act of subtle air, windy weather
song, hymn, firmament, sound, reflex	physical law of all-rays' reflex requirement, wall
release (opening) of problem [aim]	resultant feature of transition,
self	blending of subtle

7, 8, 9 (or 6) *human factor*

The source of impossible beginning of move, we know it came from "there."
It has to be possible for it to transit.
Encountering the wall, which stops or block (*physical*)
It transcends being more subtle, and have blend with elements it is passing, it brings an opening. (*subtle*)

4, 5, 6 (or 9) *personality factor*

It might come, then it might leave, then it might come, then it might leave, irregularly, unexpectedly
There is a response or resonation; do we want it or not?
We have blockage or enclosure of natural character (*physical*)
We encounter what we don't know and are standing there, not knowing what to do (*subtle*)

10, 2, 3 *transcendental*

Movement and "appearance" of what consists of subtlety, having a concrete presence.
Light-light air touch, inter-sweet, contiguity
Force of prohibition being banned and overcome without egoism

Enneagram of Significance of Conscience

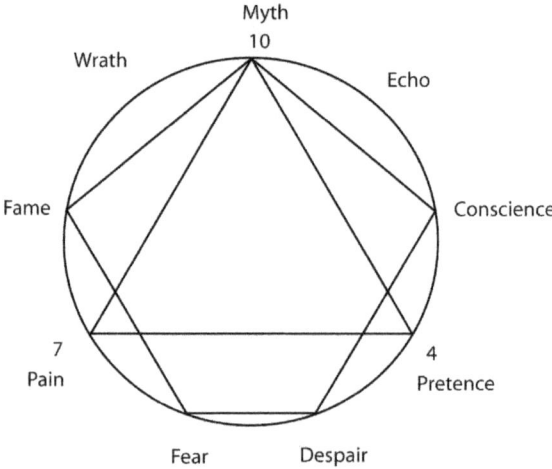

Myth	mythical creation of possible exchange; transubstantial attitude of signatures
Echo	response of knowledge on communicated arms
Conscience	pain of psyche, disillusion, OR (what can I do to get rid of both facts)
Pretence	we don't understand there really is a problem
Despair	absence of mind, communicative wire is broken, no response
Fear	complete subject to the influence of "boring" factor of someone's acts
Pain	I can't hear it anymore, it's touching, I know but how would I do

Fame	did you hear it? It's right there; let's go to look at it
Wrath	I cannot stand it to such extent that I will remove the subject

For example, something happens. The attitude is, it's going to change, and it's going to change (10). It was broadcasted there is the war somewhere, or any kind of disaster. We are under the influence of this news; we have clean feelings, and feel the heaven is nearby (2). We've seen it, and don't want it. Its very existence destroys us. We only have desire to destroy both ability to feel pain as well as its cause (3). "What are you talking about?" or "Really? What's next?" There is never participation without pretence (4). No response, no communication. One is not going to see and one is occupied (5). We see nothing except this bores us (6). I don't want to hear, because then it would touch me (7). Complete absence of any compassion (8). Annoyance and anger to such extent that we remove either what is subjected to suffer, or the reason of it (9).

As any appearance, it manifests at different times in this or that way for the same person, or we might have an inclination.

Section Two

Psychological Enneagrams with Pentagram Inside

Theorem of the Fall of Conscience

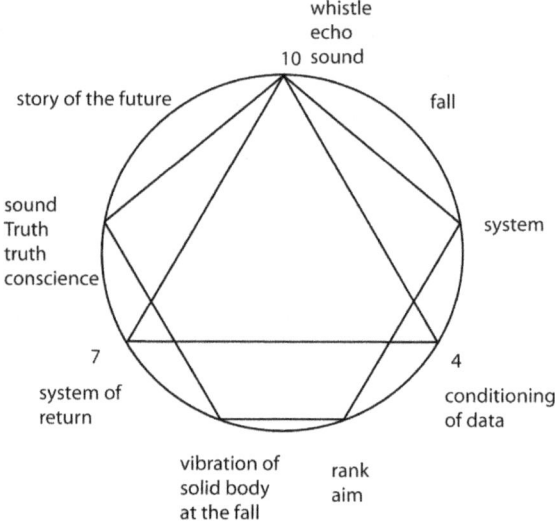

Timing Here it is fallen, what is going to be, and all this in a system. (6 9 3)

Concrete Conscience itself, its fall, and level of it (from which height it falls) (8 2 5)

Condition Distribution, system of return (responding), and conditioning of data (10 7 4)

The situation, particularities of the moment, and height.

Story of Enneagram

We live without considering the reasons of logic and mentality, but objectivity of the possible fall of conscience cannot be overestimated. Therefore, there are levels of its reaching and falling. Timing includes conditions of the fall (system), → physical vibrations of hit, → and consequences. Concrete triangle is the very conscience, how leveled it was before this, and fall. There are also factors of the world around us—of transposition of the fact and resultant of fall, reverberation, of the supposition and dating, (what it's going to be, if), and response on dispersion of sound (the subtle feature, spreading around of the loss of former height).

Theorem of Killing

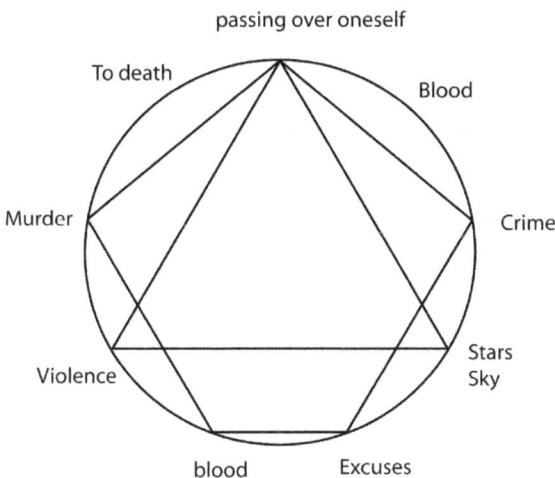

passing over oneself
violence   } timeless
stars, sky

to death
blood   } functional
crime

blood
murder   }   moral level of middle floor
excuses

We kill. Who? It doesn't really matter. We talk here of wrong doing, not for preservation, or out of defense, as it might happen. This is murder, which is done by a madman, for no real reason, without any belief of consequences. Also, it is the desire to «solve» the problem of other's living; why won't we kill, if I live and another (victim) is on his own. It is a timeless argumentation on the theme of free will, only solved by madmen. For explanation excuses are used. In a reality it's done out of hate. What is at the second stage is for a process of getting into psychological state that permits a murder. With connection to the physiology. What is wrong has a particular mental reaction; it is a crime we cannot forget others' death and blood, out of which excuses spread. Possibility to kill includes violence, passing over oneself, and feeling of «starry matter» — right of one's own significance, annoyance at having lived at all, justification of any violent action therefore.

Enneagram of the Loss of Virginity

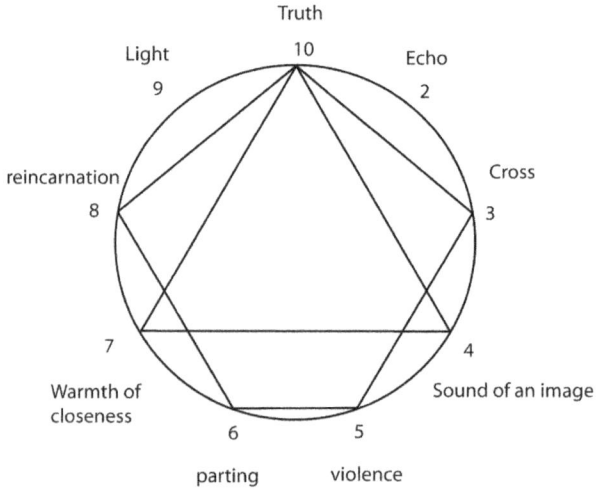

Story of Enneagram

Truth	awakening
Echo	consequences
Cross	blame, suffering
Sound of Image	representation of act, as we don't see it
Violence	should be present
Parting	separation, following the sex
Closeness	closeness at being together, warmth
Rebirth	feeling of being «incorporated» into oneself anew
Light	all holy what we might feel

10 7 4 is for the act itself

2 5 8 is for the change in a body (5), our feelings (2), and how we feel inside the body (8)

9 6 3 is for contradictory nature of every complete process; we carry obligations and issues

realization of act (10 → 4)	perception of pressure of signature factor (8 → 5)
together (5 → 7)	expression of polarities on emotional state (4 → 2)
return to truth (7 → 10)	different feeling in a new body with new sensations (2 → 8)

three steps of action: physical action, emotional participation, as well as coming out of a state.

Conditions of the Fall of Man

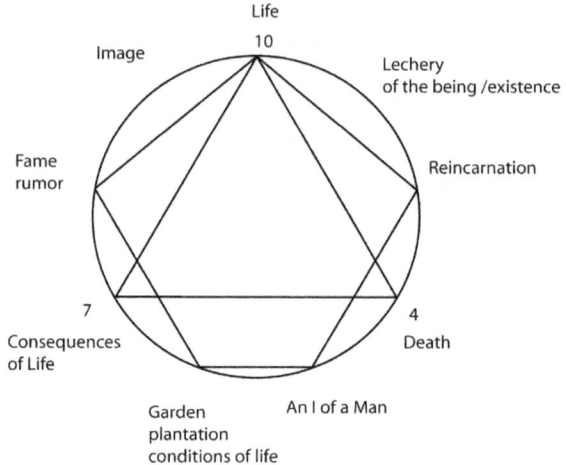

Life	Image	Recognition
Its consequences	Conditions and fruits of life	Man's I
Death	Reincarnation	Corruption of distinct

Act of living   *Inward participation*   *Output*

total process (10 → 4)   recognition depending upon realization of I (8 → 5)

individual problem & solution   dependence of what kind of death we die from being (4 → 2)

resultant factor (7 → 10)   arousal of atmosphere around life (2 → 8)

Here, image is what is following us. Conditions of life and how we work (6, garden). Real factor (3).

We are born with the qualities, and then in the process of life there appears an "image" that follows us. Our true being, or existence, could be more or less corrupted. So, it is an "outward" sign of man and inward factuality. We are born with qualities (3). During the process of our life, people around us acquire opinion of who we are. But, people themselves are different, and they cannot have one and the same idea about us, so it is called "the rumor". At the end we disappear, but there remain some consequences out of everything we've done. We do have some individual reactions, but we live in a body under certain life conditions; this also requires us to work under these regulations. In this way, the right and left parts of enneagram fall into outside and inside factors.

2, 3   are inner qualities
9, 8   are outward signature
6, 5   are result of work

Enneagram of breach of psychological health

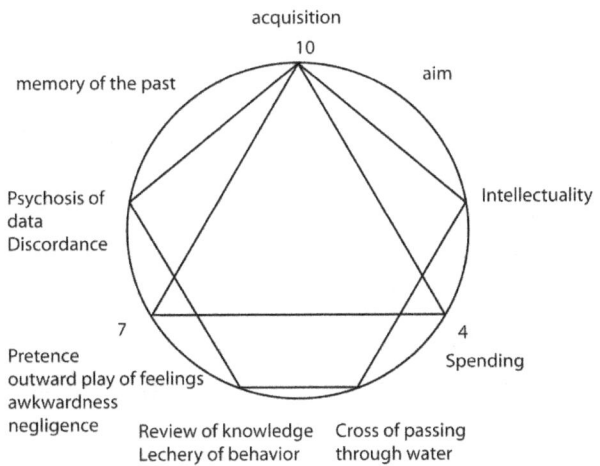

aim	intellectuality	spending
cross of passing	review of knowledge	outward play of feelings
through water	lechery of behavior	negligence
data's psychosis	passed memories	acquisition
discordance		
Controllability	*Mental factor*	*Outward factor*

This enneagram speaks about contradiction, which appears from opposing factors out of control. Being incapable to exchange the situation but by no means to agree with it, one's psychological system gets broken. Human wish is important, and if we consider the situation to be hopeless or have a lot of problems, we suffer the misbalanced state, which is just an indication of the presence of the mental feature of desire to «exchange» the situation for better, or conceal somehow what is important. We keep recurring events from the past to evaluate what happened in the intellectual, which brings the behavioral untidiness because we are occupied and don't care about what is around us. This leads to worrying about our positional unsteadiness, and we want to be constant to reach an aim for which we spent and have acquired. We act and suffer the way we believe is required for acquisition (5, pentagram). This is tension, appearing from the pressure of factors that brings up efforts out of our totality to survive our features as they are, not lose them or exchange on what «would be» more comfortable, and we are discordant with the world. This leads to pretence, sentimental flashes, awkwardness with what is around, and negligence. All this just to catch up with the possibility of acquisition. This psychological situation at which psychic stability gets broken. Stages from ten to four fall more toward activity, and those from six to nine to our reaction and inner states. Our inner state could be viewed as passive and dependent from action. The fifth stage belongs to both processes.

Enneagram of Separation

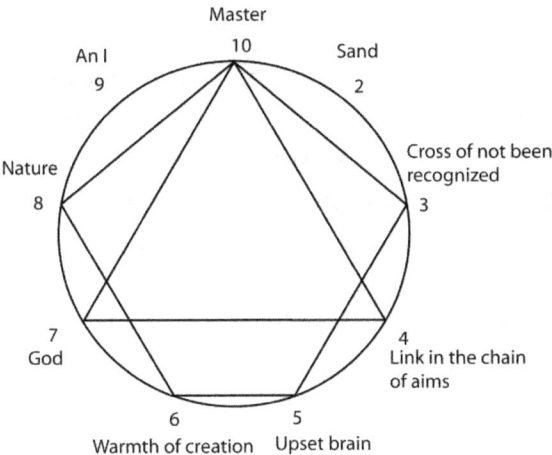

Essential of our efforts

10	what leads us
7	our deity
4	connection to

Essential of our feelings

9	me is not somewhere
6	feeling of our substance
3	situational problem inside the society

Natural reactions

2	conscious protection of reactivity, dispersion of former features not to be again
5	result of psychic instability
8	name of the man (we might have different nature, with specifics)

When we feel we are in discordance with the social interaction, we might decide emotionally to separate from what prevents us to work inside freely from the suppression, not to be the subject of some laws, but this brings also a feeling of sadness. This process includes the fact of us being offended by not being accepted as we are (3), and also physical tiredness (5) (five and six are physical-psychical factors), otherwise there is no reason for separation. There are human factors (9 and 8), as well as social (2 and 3). The character of this enneagram is that it is evolution, but out of refusal. It goes simultaneously up from 5 and 6: psychological instability and physical sensation of being full; one moment of continuous aims and what it is done for; some social problems, misunderstandings, and our personal features; finally, it is possible to separate by having our individuality and ability to «forget» whatever there was that caused our dependence. From another side, it is done because something is leading us, already for the aim of self-development, so it is at ten, as the beginning. The period could be viewed simultaneously from 10 to 4, and 8 to 5, then, etc.: from our aim we go into one of intermediate aims, and our special features cause us instability (10→4 movement toward; 8→5 breach of psychological health).

Through the reaction upon us and our reaction back we come to the possibility of separation, and having instability, we think of our deity (4→2 creation of conditions, at which we can work upon the aim, 5→7 curative action of higher influences). This makes resonance upon our features; we really feel separated, but at the same time protected, and having responded to what is upward, we come back to the initial aptitude (2→8 certain curative actions upon our psychic, change of personal features, 7→10 acquisition again, recovery); these two processes are going past stage nine, man's individuality, and have to do with its fulfillment.

Third stage is a place of interval, where additional shock is required for process to go on. These additional shocks are usually given for traditional presentation of enneagram. As here we speak about existence, it is marked down already, as if part of a set of the thing upon one level, which is correct, or it won't have connection. At this stage, suffer not being recognized, the process of separation is set up, which won't be caused by upset of psychic system only. It means, psyche isn't depressed from the reason of too big an answer toward something not really evoking it, but that we take a situation when there really is something that puts us down. Another interval comes at eighth stage, and here it is marked down so that it speaks about necessity of some addition, to overcome situation, as this stage talks of certain blockage in our feelings. Then, if it is octave, which goes down (from three), there at five there is some downward of us being unstable, but it is subdued by our common state of physical consistency.

Theorem of struggle of outward and inward character in between two carriers of separate bodies

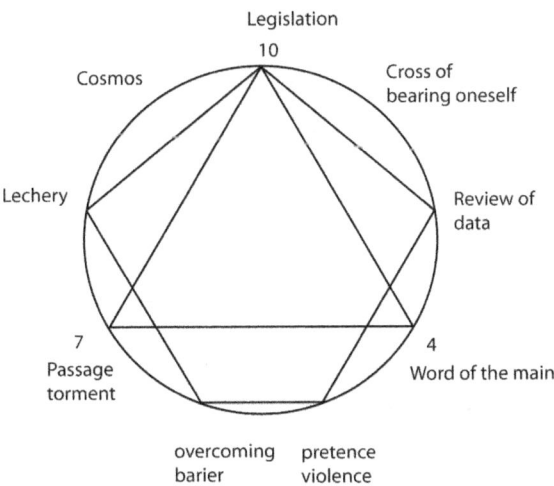

There is a possibility of conflict in between two persons. It has inner and outside reflection. There is always a question of common law (legislation), of the feeling of human rights, unspoken conscience considerations, or governmental law. Cosmos is feeling of requirement. It has to do with higher needs. They might have reflection in low levels as well. For example, keeping on time, or being polite, or fulfillment of duties, it is action. When there is a conflict there is always a feeling of inadequacy and of being suppressed; it is at the second stage, slowing down the situation, without which there would be no conflict. Lechery is impossibility to overcome one's shortcomings. Review of data is the process of gathering material of explanation of one's problems about how they proceed out of another man's actions or attitude. Word of the main is the totality of situation, in what circumstances and on what staging it is now. Whatever there is a situation, it has a particular totality. If every step of enneagram could be viewed as enneagram of itself, we can imagine here to be different stages, which correspond to some clear scheme of whatever situation. However, here it is a part of particular event, this way it isn't called just a totality of situation, but word of the main, because it speaks about this particular case. This way, situation here has particular features that correspond to all the circumstances. It involves passage through the situational factor and torment of being exposed for this experience. There is overcoming a barrier to get out into the open (or not being able to do it) and speaking up to remove it. From the side of the oppressor, there is always pretence and violence; it might be as one who is in the wrong position, who caused an inadequate situation, as well as someone who wants to remove what is caused by someone else if that was an action that annoyed them (for example, being late).

Inner triangle. Situation, what there should be, and what we experience.
Outward. Action of wrongdoing, overcoming for defence, and review of material of rights.
Inward. One's shortcomings, suffering of being oneself under this, hate.

Six and five are reactions, eight and nine are shortcomings (of persona and actions), and two and three are for being subjected.

Pentagram: feeling (10), shortcomings (8), reaction (3), action (6, 5)

Story of Enneagram

10→4 coming to the situation, contradiction
4→2   completion of way, stoppage of our own self, being touched, coming into play
2→8   *seeing* one's shortcomings
8→5   disposition, defense, or reaction upon
5→7   pressure upon the man, creation of the situation
7→10 realization of seeing the truth

Here it is *no* entry at point 8. If there would be no shortcomings, there would be no situation.

Enneagram of Fear and Feelings

10 the record of what is going on, absorption and transcribing
9   action of suppression, up to the worst
8   experience of being unsubscribed
7   content of experience
6   forceful change of us
5   memory of what is going on
4   reason of suffering
3   oppression
2   desire to die not to feel it

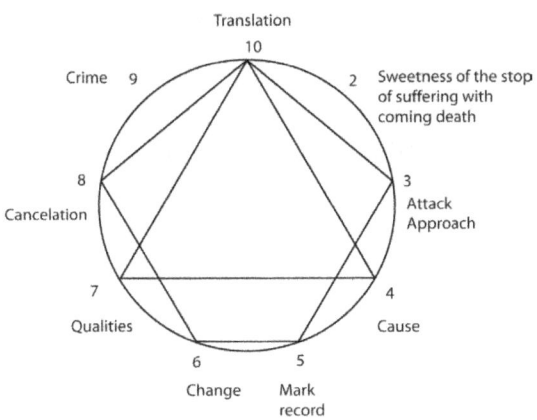

10→4   sweetness of appearance of concrete reason
4→2   complete absorption of the situation
2→8   disappearance, numbness, overdue
8→5   event
5→7   sun, coming out to seeing proceeding
7→10   realization of subscribing

This is the case, when the feeling of fear is evoked by real reasons. It includes, therefore, attack and approach for the realization of oppression, and our realization of this, the wrongdoing itself, whatever it would be, up to the criminal act and the change of it upon us, even if it is just a word, outward pressure of signature (by someone's personality), it still might be illegal. What exactly causes us suffering (4). Record, perceiving, and what is in experience. Destruction (permanent for the moment) of ability to accept the data, and reaction and «freaking out». *Functional triangle:* approach, crime, and change. *Reactional:* recording, overcoming, «passing» out. *Situational:* experience, its transcription, and coming to a reason.

From 10 to 2, stages in between corners of positioned triangle are cause and output: pressure-reaction. Act of power — disappearance; being screwed up — mark of it; approach — fear.

The process runs from 4 down. Reason —approach — fear — offence — passing out — harm — recording. Points ten and seven temporarily go out of the scheme. When the period runs from two to eight, our ability to transcribe and the content of experience are temporarily stopped. Then we come to the record of what harm had been done, and we recall what has been there. Attack and approach could be stopped at point three, then there wouldn't be such enneagram. There would be a stop of attack, shot to stop, disqualification (10), and escape.

Enneagram of Violence

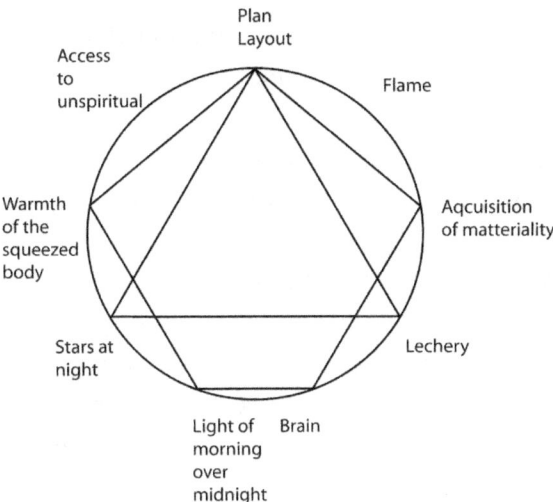

2, 5, 8   *Physical factor*
9, 6, 3   *Unspiritual fact*
10, 7, 4   *Corruption*

Cryptograph of film about war.

corruption of feelings (9)
disposition of facts in life (how and what happens) (12)
adulation (11)
qualification of wonder (14)
echo of triumph (15)
communication (20)
whistle of the devil (8)
story of love and fame of primogeniture (11)
smell of love and story of null (10)
quit, I leave, it's absent, all is lost, come down soon, I am the cloud of love, no one would touch me, because I am out. (12)
sweet time forever, now we are done (14)
warmth of love and fame of primogeniture (15)

task of the main and summer of deity(7)
cry of the god, to forget (12)
warmth of love and fame of understanding (16)
patience of main and cloud of some (13)
whatever is it, all is so-so (14)
crime of the main and gold of love (15)
strong is embrace, rumor is not a hindrance (6)

Creation of violence happens by certain layout. Each stage could be viewed as a single enneagram, connected with totality of process. To distinguish stages of inner enneagrams, they are given other sets of numbers; each stage is an example of the inner pentagram. They go as 10-8-3-6-5, sum of all the numbers gives together by addition the number of the stage. Example: 12+11+14+15+20=72; 7+2=9, ninth stage. These numbers have correct meanings of traversing each stage. They are connected in between by certain law, which has nothing to do with logic or outcome of forces; it is just concern of the future to realize the possibility of it to be seen.

Corruption of Feelings (access to unspiritual).

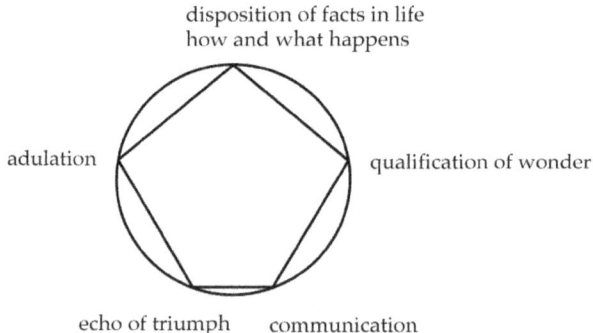

We can understand that this is invariably involved as a need not to have concern of other people's needs and of having nice-working functions in the situation and position when one has only cried. What used to work at peaceful times has to continue to work. This way, we have communication (of what is around), adulation, or it won't work, assumption of happiness (echo of triumph), amusement, enough not to feel on its own, and ten has the «beginning»— common fact—just a disposition of events, and what it is about. We can see that triad of 9-6-3 is about feelings, and 2-5-8 is functional of operating.

The numbers, which are used for inner octaves, speak about the same truth, if they are marked by one and the same figure.

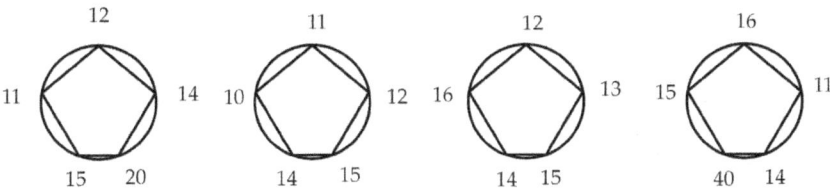

All numbers are connected by a chain of links of consequences; it is meaningful in the content of a particular subject, and another subject would give different combinations of the meaning. These secondary enncagrams suppose to answer in nature to the bigger process to which they belong. Here the titles are given for the stages of the pentagrams for some of these. They are marked in terms or expressions that would suggest a similar atmosphere and abstract idea (image) of this particular phenomenon. A different term might be applied as well, or as an explanation and clarification of a subject. My nature is fluidity. It is polite to overcome around, like this. In this way, anything might be expressed, up to the difficult (complicated) subjects, what is required is a particular freedom of mentation, otherwise one speaks in terms of functional requirements and quality and deeper belonging is missed and forgotten. It is not impossible to uncover wrongness of existential qualities. What is impossible is to believe that everything that is possible to know is already known. What is before people at this time is the search for sentences, which would explain right away, as a statement, one particular truth or legal communicative feature in between people for social interaction. What is in the operation now is logic. We use all sets of words for it, but not everyone could operate successfully even in this set. There is never a possibility of anything to come out that would «save» the world, would bring salvation in terms of social stability; but society should operate more or less successfully for possible freedom and common participation, otherwise we have people dispersed and not connected in between. We now have to belong to the world of enterprise. What is difficult is its continuation in the same totality of factors; it is gonna slow down. What is going to take its place is going to be seen at its time. We never realize consequences as well as change, which happened; what we see is just one slice of three-dimensional space (in abstract), expressed as a two-dimensional representation, taken at a given time. World CHANGES. It could be called deception to give any direction, go there, you will find, as long as there is no us, there is none. As long as there are we, it is danger. Danger of loss, danger of being exchanged, and fear. And the desire to deceive the doom. Violence doesn't have any considerations or feelings in terms of how I would react, what it is for me, how it breaks my life, it rather includes happy features of «getting out», «rid», deception, receiving, survival, victim whose life is broken is not there, no his output, who he is, and why he is important, it (of v) is just egoistic. Pretence, molecule of wrongness, ever and everywhere, a deception of possibility to live well through its «overcome», overcome of anything, to stiff the world for not dangerous existence.

Interesting. We could've suggested that if there is egoism, in the future there also would be violence. And our personal freedom is always unstable, we are scared for its destruction. We have never understood the implication of flight. What walls are gonna change it, etc. You can use any terms, but bad, it happened being of violence.

Mask is important for consideration.

Who will kill me, if I have died.

Suggestion is unimportant, everything which is going on is just conditioning, not quite, because there are requirements, of what is comfortable, good for health. We should've chosen. What is good, we weren't raped today. No possibility of survival, I don't know. Is it possible to go on? Probably, but in a different setting.

Come to me, I'm flight,   sounds more poetic and
Lesson of the high,   could've be used for something else, etc.

This is unimportant. We are left with decision to communicate truth, required for human interaction, but this supposes there is a better way of explanation «what I feel, what I am». How could it be? As long as there are no certain meanings, there are no explanations. It's insignificant, or is it? Your choice, but it is just a picture of what we are; we could've make things better but we are scared to make them worse. To be in certain terms with world is easy. To be exact is very unfair.

Was it just a number of sentences, or is there a meaning behind it?

Picturing Enneagrams

Enncagram of Tune of Image of the Sound

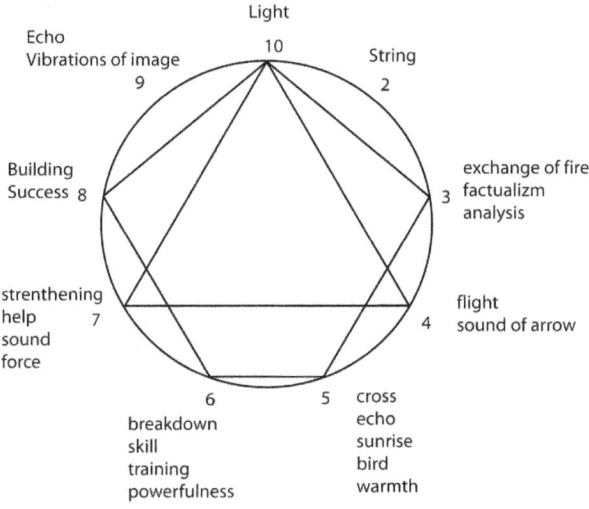

Sound might have an image. We hear a noise and our abstract ability translates it into some image. This image has a certain meaning. So, we take an abstract subject to go around enneagram.

9	reaction upon this "representation"
8	erection of meaning
7	reason to go on
6	how good we are at discrimination
5	representation
4	space, distance in abstract and factual
3	what is it? should we answer?
2	level and source
10	objectivity, how true it is, significance of it on its own, not someone's reaction

Sound → first reaction — how far is it? (distance)
Have discriminated distance → we are discriminating its level and what is it out of (2)
Knowing what's the nature, we → make up the common meaning
Having the meaning we move to representation (8→5)
Representation moves us to go on.
Activity leads us to objective.

It doesn't matter, would we approach the source of noise, is it a word on which we should react and answer, is it order, warning, an expression of happiness, mechanism of accepting the sound is one and the same.

If we lose the hearing, all the mechanics give a strange shock to the body at not being capable of answering its usual way. So, it's not only reaction, it is also experience, which is lost and is accepted as a natural quality of happiness and joy. For this reason are used expressions that speak up for us of natural uprisings, like a bird and sunrise, because these answer the subject.

Enneagram of Going Behind the Boundary

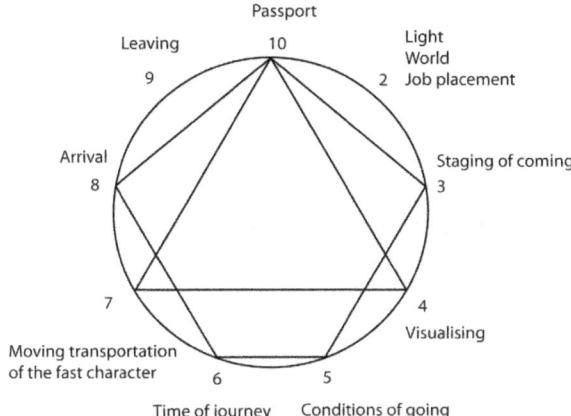

Visualizing — Time of journey — Passport — Staging of coming — Transportation — Arrival — Passport (custom) — Conditions of travel (going in the past) — Visualizing (of leaving and back to the situation — to the job, daily basis.)

8 – one should arrive then it is complete
4 – one has to wish to go

Enneagram of Manifestation

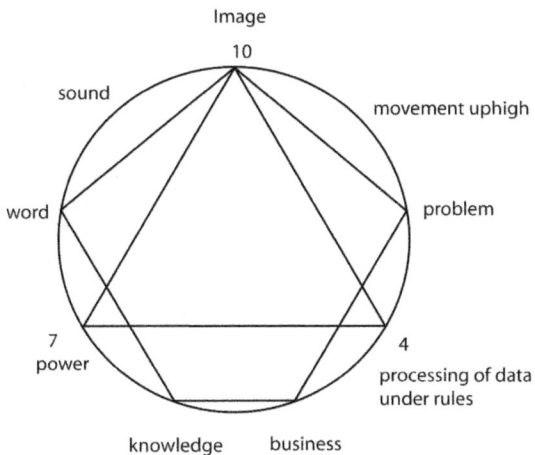

Image	Individuality
Sound	Perception
Word	Manifestation
Power	Energy
Knowledge	Mind
Action	Function
Processing of data under rules	Assimilation
Task	Intelligence
Movement up high	Will

Power → Image = Result (processing of data in correspondence to the image)

Movement upward → Action = Word (word as a result and manifestation of self in the flow of solving of process (action)

Perception → mind = intelligence
Sound → knowledge = problem
Task appearing in mind in result of what was seen

Problem of Divination

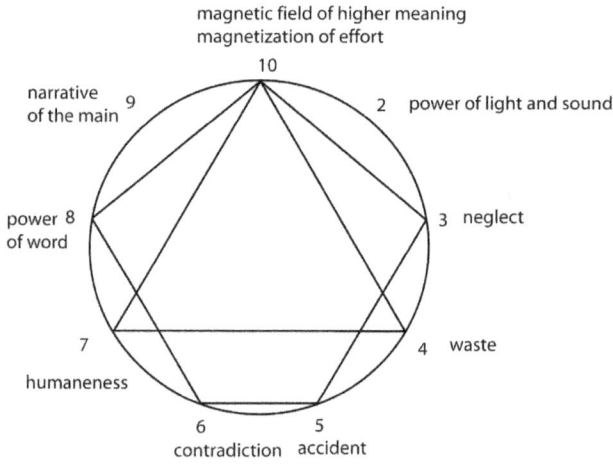

History of art	9
Literature, fiction, documentary	8
Philosophy	7
Military	6
Society	5
Jail, court	4
School, institutes	3
Musical issue, dramatic effect, theater	2
Occultism	10

Another example:

artistic field, astronomy
writing, poetry
aspiration, Christianity
no military service
being antisocial
being in trouble, losing license
unfinished education, credits
preference of rock music
no occult features, curative acts, etc.

Enneagram of Help

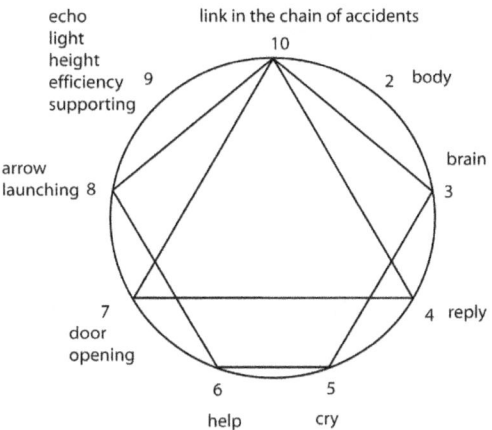

body, brain – physical factors
help, cry – emotion
nine and eight – conscious efforts

happening—answer, reaction—exit

If we need help, it is supporting (9), this position also includes its capacity and level of waves. Indication and direction of line to intention. (8)
Exit (7)
Saving act (6)
Ask for help (5)
Answer, gratitude (4)
Communication (3)
Physical support (2)

This is enneagram, which has pentagram, but there is a "hidden" period of another pentagram. In this way, we see the function here upon the scheme in its existential capacity, but all the stages also include in them a possible process, which isn't existential, of mechanical proceeding because there is another enneagram overlapping it with stages where nine can be imagined to be at ten, so that it is body—cry—brain, etc.

Body – Cry (being in the physical state and asking for help, therefore, 1→4 of hidden enn is coming into the situation, which requires help);

Cry – Brain (asking for help and communication, so 4→2 is producing our inner cry into output and issue);

Brain – Echo, Efficiency, Supporting (communication and support; we address the thing up high to descend to us 2→8 realization of insufficiency);

Echo, Support – Help (8→5 producing possibilities to take one out of circumstances).

This is the end of the period of hidden enn (in this scheme).
From another side, our cry and asking for help, through the help (6), leads to the exit, and from it we come back to the next stage of the situation.
In this way, there are two sets of octaves from which one begins, and not coming to the end, and another begins out of it and finishes up the process.
It is hard to realize the possibility of anything to be as they are.
Possibility of hidden enneagrams to exist as they were is that things overlap; we see the scheme, including stages that are required by their nature and distributed around the circumference with the connections in between them as they are. This depends upon the nature of process.

PART
TWO

Section One

Individual Enneagrams

Enneagram of Fortunate Overcoming of Work

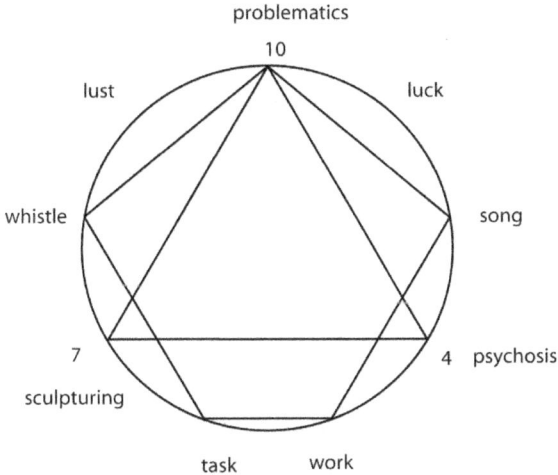

Complete action requires a fortune (luck)
It is done with breaks (whistle)
There is the task
Tuning to the work is required for successful production (song)
Inclination and disturbance (lust)
Problematic of the whole job
I won't have the capacity or ability to do this (psychosis)
Bond of things together and application of form (sculpturing)

8, 9 is out of order label
6, 5 is for action and functional direction (what exactly)
2, 3 is for alternative and capacity

Even though it is a personal scheme, it could be applied to any similar process.

Problematic is the question at hand. What we do, we separate the work process as it is with its requirement of taking a break and «lucky findings» with complicate feature of our own factor of being disturbed and necessity to be tuned to the theme of the job—the immediate task. Difficulty is, we need to overcome our elemental factor and give the form to common process, receive stabilization and fluidity, and then the problem is solved and the task is accomplished. We can take it higher, where tuning is achieved for all the automatic requirements; now we are high, without any process getting along with research or activity, day after day in a spinning wheel.

Enneagram of Contradictory Emotions

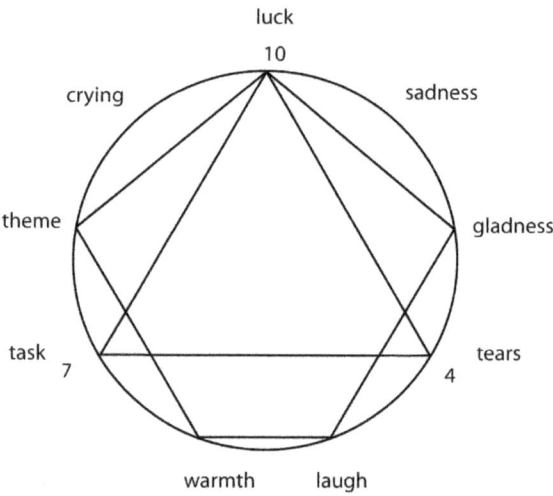

Story of Enneagram

This is enneagram of contradictory emotions; it falls into three orders of "positive" em, negative, and [salvation]. If to uncover reasons for which they took the places they do upon the scheme, inner "work" of "hidden" factors, making up at least this enneagramatic photo, would have clarification.

7	8	9	10	2	3	4	5	6
task	theme	crying	luck	sadness	gladness	tears	laugh	warmth
solve	solve	no	solve	no	yes	no	yes	yes

In this way we can see the pattern of positive and negative answers with a solution.

Example:

warmth	having ideal
laugh	sweetness of pleasure
tears	being disturbed
gladness	peaceful pacification
sadness	inward realization
luck	coming upon thread
crying	loosing everything
theme	pacification through involvement
task	having a next point of decision

Enneagram of Failing Discovery

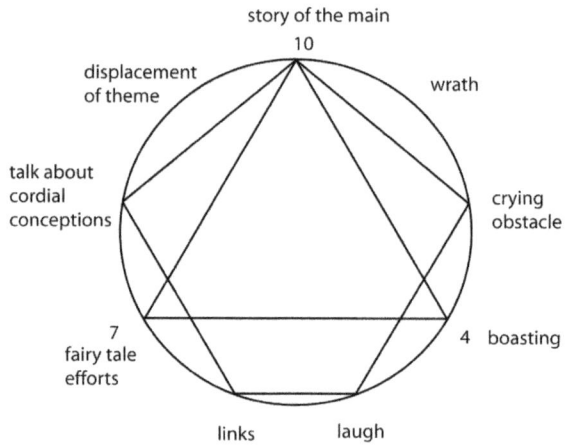

10	main feature of corruption
9	it wasn't that, now it's about this
8	sentimentality
7	efforts toward nonexistent successful achievement
6	what should lead toward the goal, deceptive info
5	contempt to both efforts and failures
4	I gonna do this again
3	coming to impossibility accomplish
2	disaster and efforts to overcome, with emotions

These are automatic reactions based upon false concepts, giving a result that is a repetition of efforts with illusionary aims, result, and map of interactions. At the base of it stands mistaking opinion of oneself so that the total scheme flows out of it; no time for recurrence is allowed to subtract the features of the mistaking idea as recipient is having a knowledge of ones own mistakes pretty well but sees no option of subsiding outlines of ones own self. This diagram pictures a phenomena of work that necessary brings to failure. This happens because person who makes effort doesn't have ability. The reasons for someone's incapability aren't given, and they are supposed to constitute a secondary enneagram, at stage ten. That is, if to look up tenth stage as an enneagram itself, there should also be explanations or some kind of remarks about the reasons. There could've enter self-concern, possibly with attachment of what made one to have a weak character, ignorance, believe that things go correctly, barriers making a disillusion in illusory perspective of things to be unreachable. If these features are in work, they give the one who works like this a pleasure to think, plan, and work upon it (9, 8, 7). But the efforts are real and bring, by the scheme, real results — an inability to make it work (3), with all the emotion corresponding to the character of bearer. To make the scheme work, we need the main feature, and existence of wrong information (6), it is a "negative" illusion with real efforts, so the scheme works, but not.

After looking over three different "personal" enneagrams about achievement, could be seen that each of them has its characteristic route to the goal. In the first process, it is an application of one's approval to action, where results are achieved. At the second case, goal appears out of being unable not to have a goal at these conditions. In the third there is "invention" of the goal, exchange of true for a substitute. In the first example, task is as if given. In the second aim, the very task is reliable. What we need to understand is that every scheme works with its own factors; there are no other factors to enter. In the first one, there is a particular inability of character, which should be, and which is possible, to overcome for good management. But still it would give only a possible production out of a work process. What is in subject is the stabilization of the process for the regular and successful job, without too big of being jerks. In second, it is instability of feelings, but the very job is not a problem, it's not difficult, all feelings go toward achievement. However, it is about a certain illusion to bring the sweetness ever-ever this task, even accomplished, cannot. Third is a ruin of the work, and results don't come up, but there is no realization that it was initially impossible, that plan was a fake one. There are efforts, but they don't bring results or don't bring what was expected. As we see, it is not functional; we talk about processes achieved by people, having characteristic outlines of positions of features, which we don't discuss. Psychological poses are an example; we don't discuss "possible" situations of which we do not know. However, certain types of personality, as well as situations, could be recognized, just because they are taken from a realistic frame.

We never know what is coming up. However, it is not difficult to see a recurrent feature of inability or ability to achieve the aim. Still, there are our personal features present. Should we or shan't we overcome this? We need to remember that there is not a sterile world around us; our aims, wishes, loss, requirements, and possibilities make up our life, which we would like to see be better. What we talk of is the application of efforts and what it speaks of. First scheme talks about the flow of process. We need to bring in all desirable elements. There are no suppositions, we are all together in a process, because it requires from one to tune to it in order it would go on. At the second, we occupy with task, believing, it's giving an exit, but it is illusion. We occupy with it very close, till the next problem comes up. This problem won't arise neither from us nor what we've been doing. This way, we didn't get out of it. What could be done? Third is just pacification of conscience, with the help of falsity of information and infrequency of thought.

What is required is not a requirement. The possibility of achievement of aim, in any case difficult, is dangerous and involves our pacification of inward qualities of wrong up-hilling, never before managed by actions whatsoever. Even if struggle toward the aim does bring ability, it is due to reasons outside of functional mechanic set, it is us who chose the thing, how we manage inside the situation, and what are the processes that lead to it. If we don't observe ourselves apart from situation and even our personal attractions we won't realize what really is taking a place. Our feelings always need to be involved, when we occupy, so we would never make a barrier in between of us and proceeding because we belong to it. It is wrong to think that we can just "decide" do this or that, and we would receive results. A difficult feature of there being inward octaves and requirements of "shocks" in designated places includes a compilation of an altogether settlement of actions, situations, involvement, wishes, and desires, which we cannot choose to subside, cut out, or what, from whatever point of view; if we are cold, we are wrong already — a very different outlook from what is usually supposed by common business achievements, or even presupposed by a particular quality of a person, otherwise there wouldn't be any problem for anyone to achieve whatever road we've chosen. No, there is always a problematic, issued from our own self — do we want it or not — and there is no happiness in action. The very action is problematic. It is as are we capable or not, so and the subject we long to work upon. Any issue should be solvable. In theory whoever we are, we can exchange. If there is something wrong in us, it is mistake, which could be "cured" if we want.

Theorem of Creation of Personality

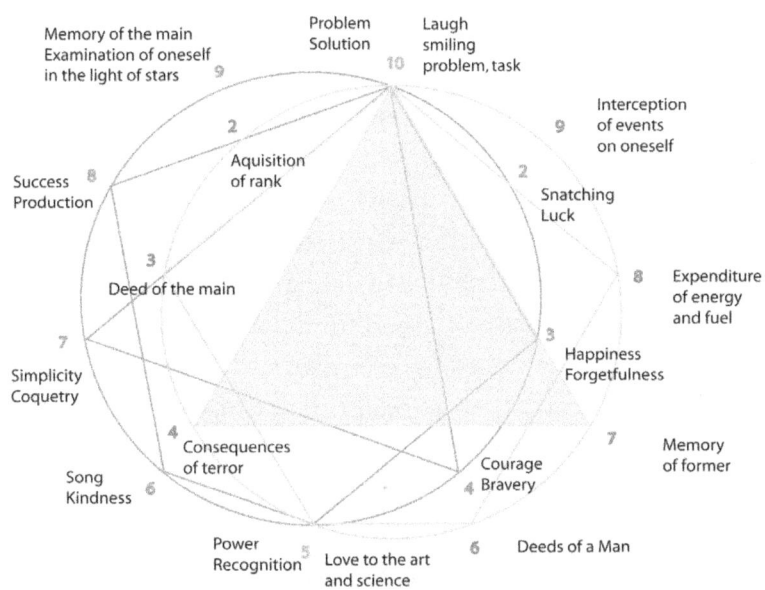

Problem, solution	Laugh, smiling, problem, task
Memory of the main	Interception of events on oneself
Success, production	Expenditure of energy and fuel
Simplicity, coquetry	Memory of former
Song, kindness	Deeds of a Man
Power, recognition	Love to the art and science
Courage, bravery	Consequences of terror
Happiness, forgetfulness	Deed of the main
Snatching, luck	Acquisition of rank

This is an example of created life interactions made possible by true judgment and proceeding (transformation) of qualities; therefore we see here two enneagrams, one preceding, and one "developed," or aspired to the high, (so that it is aslant), connected with the first one by the link of consequences. How well it could be done, it might be tried to make connections and clarify main points of interactions, even though it is personal, not linked with us. For example, in simple processes we can discern certain characteristic features. So in a bigger process there should be main, courageous acts of power and belonging, if it is about "overcoming" and transformation. We can see that even in the first one there are qualities, which speaks of a former problem but also lead to further involvement. In some of the stages there are opposite factors, as at number 10 of second enn, and also such things, which are very difficult to observe what would require few schematic enneagrams for full clarification as something already managed to be accomplished. We talk here of the man in general terms. However, we can approach someone else situation from objective side. As long as it takes, there are requirements, for example, such things as acquisition of rank, or qualification, also, deeds of the main or situation and procedure. Deeds of Man is what and who one is, it should fall in concern as well. There are also quite personal features as love to the art and science, and consequences of terror; it means one had to pass through problems. It speaks also about the future where what used to prevent have been removed. Then, it is only a recollection. Interception of events on oneself is acquired ability, which also speaks of conscious drive. This place might have in it longing, intuition, and relation. Ten is also fairly personal freedom to what one belongs. It combines such different things as one's emotions and also the task. It is common to spend energy on work, but here it also talks about personal drive toward the goal on which it's getting spent. It is self-requirement of giving oneself up to what one works upon. Still, it is not a portrait because all main features are absent, but this schematic thing tells of a possibility of density; it is not simplicity or an act of power, there is "a lot of it." There is also the memory of former; what tells of belonging and realization.

In the next, big schematic particle of this, we can see completely different qualities; it is flight out of former self up and away, but still the same situation is present, only reactions are different. There is happiness and forgetfulness—two factors, which are predisposed for each other, as a release from bondage of actions or pressure, there are mostly pairs, which are speaking of former belonging to the process and overcoming it. This way, we miss the totality of actions, which leads to pacification of self-features and the acquisition of the ability to work in any setting. So, there are snatching and luck, problem and solution, success and production. Particular qualities of someone are seen at the way for example, at one step there are combined simplicity and coquetry, and at another song and kindness. Such compilation should've belonged to someone in particular. Some one else might not develop it together, it's a type of personality. By this way, we can see that it is not only a scheme of "creation of personality," it is just an example of one man. Our reaction on it is just a personal matter. What we see here is *His* reactions on us, as courage and bravery. His only reaction on himself is at number nine, of examining oneself under starry light. It might seem like too much, but we take an example of something simple, however in complicate and multifaceted interactive activity and stabilization, which might speak of bigger problems and solutions that we don't know of. Humanity of situation is not only connected with artistry of outer figurative demand, but with forceful acts of necessary reaching toward the exchange of life's qualities around as they touch us. We can see at the points of connection how an exchange of qualities to deal with or reactions happened. Instead of having himself together with the task, we already have a problem and solution. We can think of it in terms of qualities, so that it would become clear that if something is good, then its production would bring success. Or, there is power and recognition, not power and aggression, so that speaks about banal quality of peacefulness yet importance. What is at hand is the significance of outcome. It is not an easy interactive scheme; it connects us with the problem of any human enterprise, yet with substitution of something toward the goal; instead of "just me," it is the creation of personality. There is controversy in between the one and the world, and one cannot be completely indifferent, he struggles for his way.

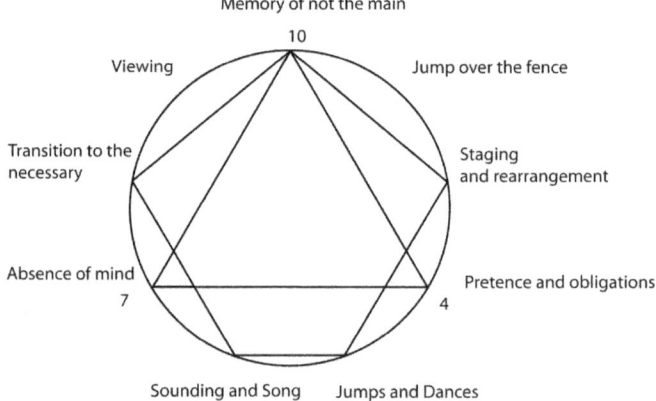

Theorem of Ease

This is a theorem of ease, which the title presupposes that something was come up toward the main. 9 and 8 is aim, 5 and 6 is means, 2 and 3 is attitude. Then, 3, 9, and 6 is a triad of Hope. 2, 5, and 8 is Carriage. 10, 4, and 7 is play role.

In this way, we can see the totality of process of being easy toward transactions. It doesn't mean this does not include work, but it is done in a particular way. We can perceive conditioned freedom in actions. This means there is some kind of barrier not just to not be involved and have impartial perspective, but a barrier itself is part of the possibility to do this. In this way, particular terms are used like at second and fourth stages.

When viewing and transition to necessary (eighth and ninth stages) could be called intentional, jump over the stage and staging and rearrangement (second and third stages) are for the activity. The content is exemplified at fifth and sixth stages. The frame of it is particular attention, paid toward what isn't the subject of a real goal.

Intermission

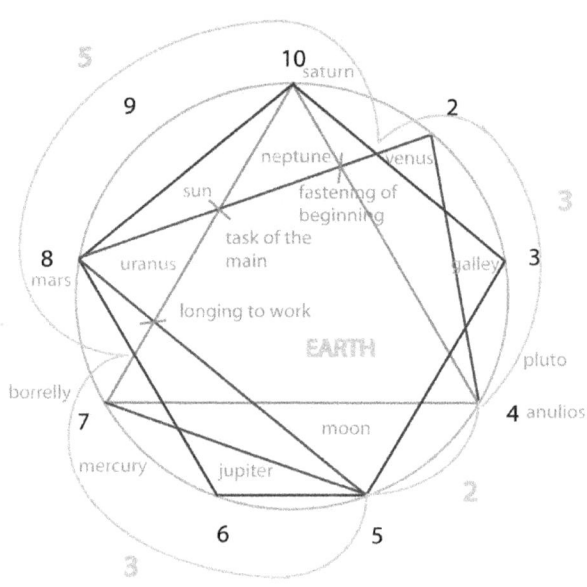

Thirteen influences compared to the solar system

(0)	Anulios	4	(11)	Borrelly	7
(10)	Moon	5			
(2)	Mercury	7	(9)	Pluto	4
(3)	Venus	2			
(12)	Galley	3			
(4)	Mars	8	(6)	Saturn	10
(7)	Uranus	8	(8)	Neptune	10
(13)	Sun	9			
(5)	Jupiter	6			

We can rearrange the scheme so that it would bring attention to certain qualities in the universe, which are hard to discern further. In any case, there should be a universal matter of existence, acquiring certain qualities, and therefore living over some plan of over-consideration (supra-staging). It is stellar. What action could bring it? It doesn't matter. The fact remains that there is objective power of artificiality of static. Dynamism arises later out of static stabilization. In this way, we can imagine the scheme, balanced in its parts in between themselves with unknown qualities. Difficulty is in not putting it down to a low level of functional stuffing; it is not that, or seeing it in the perspective of "our" world, because it is limited. What it could be applied to might be what is called, *the planetary influences*, of which, as I wrote in the first published by me book, there are thirteen, but I have connected those with the character of planets; and, in fact, planets themselves bear those very influences as a type. It has to do with vibrations, whatever place in the universe, of whatever galaxy, whatever time, any concentration might have these planetary influences; there is only this number with their qualities of vibrations, which might be imagined by colors as well, as I did so in self-published writing, "*Enneagram in Color*", where I included this idea of planetary types, in its factuality of having these or that type, corresponding in totality to something like a chord.

This way, there is something like a practically unknown art of vibrations, which we can raise and use by this way of associative power. Here, I wrote these rising concentrations as planets' names, each for each triangle, trying to make as better sense as I could, have put the sun at 9, for the "longest" by its base triangle, etc.

There are also three "fastenings." It is out of the inner quality of things. They talk of longing, aim, and primogeniture, because everything would be senseless without these. Scheme relates only to existence in its natural qualities of wonderment and polar interactive currency, through the frame of contemplation, which should not be forgotten.

If there are other sets to which this "law" could be applied, we might know these, or not. Possibly it is what always was connected with the planets — chakras or metals — but it is the same thing of vibratory nature, with its characteristic polarities. We might wish not to think in terms of limitations, but this is what it looks like, as a barred enclosure, because there are only these influences.

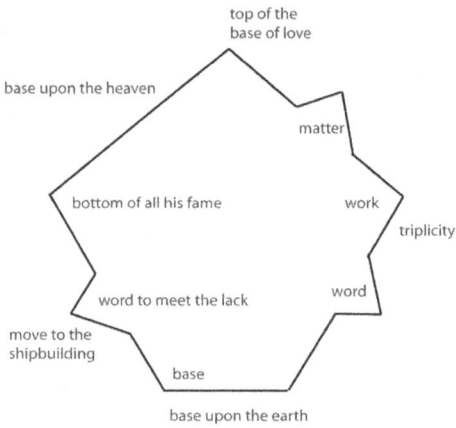

Top of the base of love
Bottom of all his fame
Word of remembrance
Base
Physical world

Word
Work   } triplicity
Matter

Base upon the heaven
Base upon the earth

Outline of total figure lets view it in consistency. It is not an actuality, it is the scheme, which takes stages and connection in between them in cosmological terms.

Section Two

Part One

Enneagram of Repetition of Knowledge

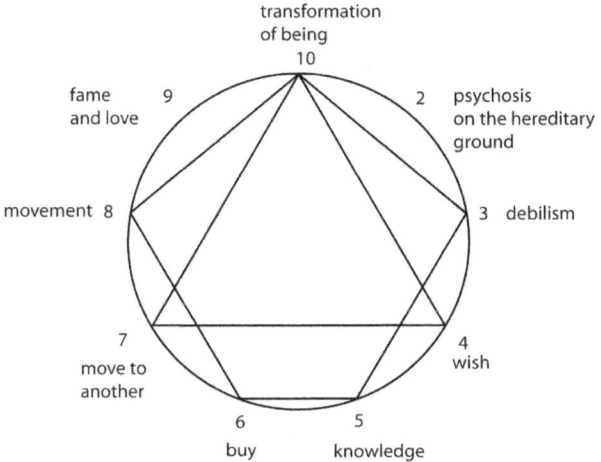

Transformation of being comes through the accumulation of fine elements, which are gathered by magnetic pull (4). There is exchange (7); it means some movement toward, not stagnation, because one cannot dip from one and the same lake; it is also governed by wish. We have prehistory, which is at two. Three is acquisition-of upbringing. The very fact of knowledge (5). Six is necessary action when to acquire, one pays for this. The very fact of movement (8), not of direction of move (7). Research brings to choice where what is recognized or loved by us is chosen (9).

Enneagram of Repetition of Action and the End of Love

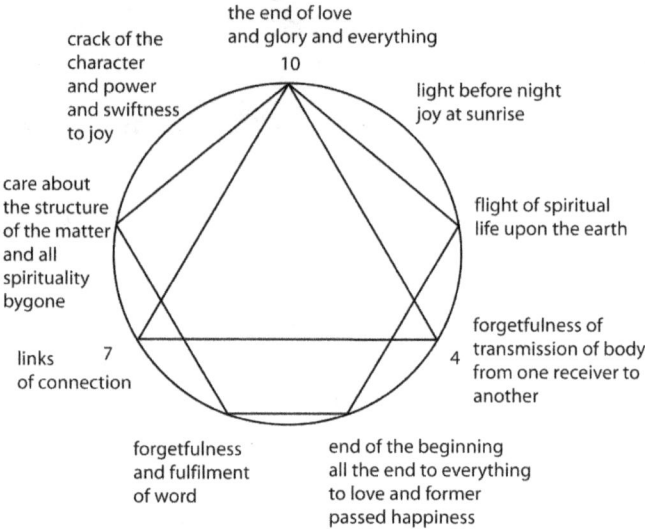

This enneagram is dedicated to our feeling of inadequacy of transmitting love into our powers of interactivity with the world around us. We have here the same nine-cyclic interactive scheme as everywhere when the process is put together accordingly to the requirement of all parts to be present. What is it? It is not only about the process in totality, because the subject is difficult for perception. We know we feel it. Stages are requirements for the action to be, not just connected in between feelings, accidental and not processed. If taken with inner octaves, they might be explained better to totality of process, and why these different participatory parts work together as well and their appraisal. It is not only why the subject takes this position for a stage, it is also of *why* is it that it takes place at all, and what is it that we feel. There are also terms used, which would be characteristic for the feeling, or mood, of the subject. Let us consider that what is at stage ten is on the order higher. It also should be the primary beginning. Here it is that we feel the world is done, so it is the end of love. It is often an experienced feeling. You see, we move around the world and our life continues, so, even if it is the end of love, we continue to walk the streets — we need to get up the next morn for school, work, etc. Outside we cannot permit it to be seen. This way, it is done, but action continues its repetition. At the sequential line, is it a descending or ascending process? It is not phenomenon, not arising either, it is the process in our emotions, but it's connected with processes in the world around us. The point of the triangle at stage four is a connection of our feelings; it is inadequacy in terms of the fact of being in a dream state when we don't understand our requirements. One doesn't know who he is. What he feels is a feeling of emotionally being opened. On another side, at seven, it is links of connection, because otherwise we are dispersed. Knowledge of the situation, not in its totality but in its disconnectory feature — that we walk the street and that we would get up — this disconnection holds us together. Our feeling would be incomplete and wouldn't make any sense if there wouldn't be the feeling of separation. This separation is perceived in feelings as presentiment in actuality, because we already feel it, not of happiness but of being free at suffering. This is exemplified by the slogan light before night, joy at sunrise. Here it is a collision of circumstance and desire. In the mentality we experience it as a blockage, so that there is a crack in the character=from outside we continue to walk, and inwardly we are suppressed. Stages three and eight, where there are places for intervals, talk about consequences for us out of totality of the process of consideration of *how* we are gonna live with it with these feelings. We know, we continue everything, but it is also a question of us to continue, and the result is it becomes for us unspiritualized because we care now only for processes to continue, so it is care about structure of the matter — are the dishes done, have we washed our hands, etc. For our participation for inward requirements, it is not that we don't care, but we feel that there is flight of spiritual life; it is a feeling of movement, in a way, and it is the preparation for future renewal of it, so that it saves itself with this. At the fifth stage, it is half of ten, so it is the end of the beginning, the end of love, world, etc. What is different from the tenth stage is that at ten it is an example of what it is about; here it is detailing, it is the end of a particular beginning, the fact it transpired, and also it is not an end to glory, it is an end of our personal happiness we had been having. Six is a point of subsiding, so it is a necessary factor of us being in a kind of haze, or we wouldn't be able to stand it, or would see reasons, but we are not, so what occurred, we were predisposed to this feeling (of enn's subject), and this happened.

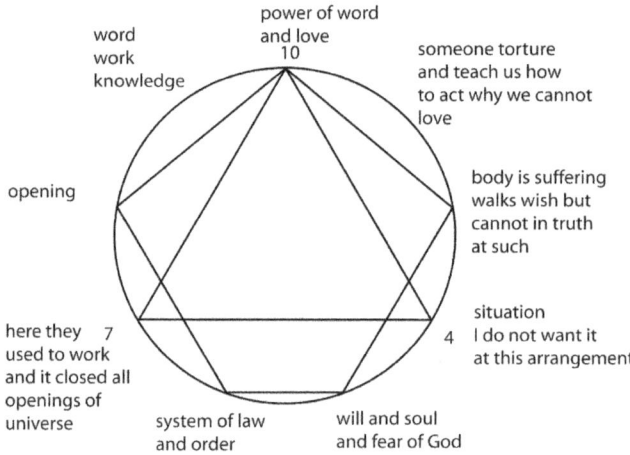

Enneagram of Failed Connection

Let us discuss psychological processes at filed connection. We have here the initial subject of falling in love, but as ten, it is a spiritual fact of existence of love and its power to guide, so it is power of word and love. This supposes that at the base there is a reality of spiritual part, a response toward something highest. However, we should understand that we talk of a situational problem. Then, we consider the case when it is failing. Therefore, it is not an initial meaning that is no good; it is the situation. This way it is pressure at stage two. So, we see no development of relationships already. The meaning of the title at the second stage is it is someone's pressure, immediate or prior. Out of this factor, we have our common state, after there is no evolvement of our feeling; if it is suppressed inside, we suffer, but we cannot do this at this situation, which is pointed out at a fourth station. This way, it is the point (a beginning of the octave, we feel the pull), then a prearranged thought, physical-emotional state, and situation. At five it is now addressing what is up-high, but from the point of view of inability. We explain with this why is it so from a point of view of justification of things, and there may be no reason for not manifesting or inability, so that this turning toward what is high is already of involuntary falsification, substitution of meaning, invariably evoked because of our total state of inability and weakness toward the situation, with outwardly pressing suppressed inwardly feelings. Six is now system of law and order, if at five, we make an address and connection, in expectation of bigger pressure to what is important, this is a transition toward just how things proceed in generality; yes, there are reasons. There was no action, so we are now under common influence. Our universe is not sterile, there is a place for egoism; if we do not have it but have no protection, and we are under limitation of possibilities. At eight it is opening. This happens for the reason that nothing lasts eternally, sooner or later it is done, and we get out. Then it is word, work, and knowledge, you see, if it is about filed connection, totality cannot bear our sentimental exemplification of tears toward, etc., moreover, it is a passed experience already, and we move toward ourselves. This brings us to the realization that if it is a true feeling, at least the very feeling, not a subject, we invariably get into such situations because if we are capable, it is *us* in question, not anything else, either we have it, or not, and then we are stuck in situational pressure and being restricted.

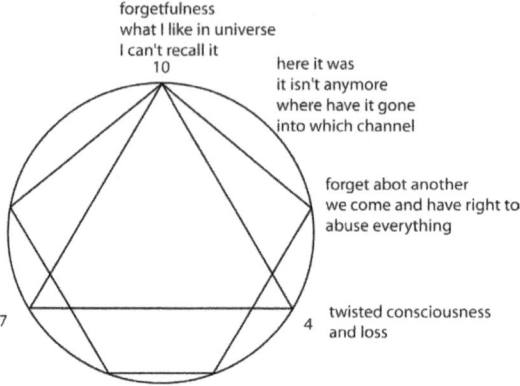

Unfinished Enneagram

This is unfinished enneagram, so it has no title. There is opinion to survive by act. Directory is our wish. When we forget what we like, there is no reason. So, this used to be, but is absent now. We can search for it. Three — entry, not only us, someone might have no problem in acting, and we are suppressed with our desire to find out. Then, it is twisted consciousness and loss. We can continue, but it is not of big importance.

Part Two

Enneagram of Responsiveness of "Feeling" of Blood Belonging

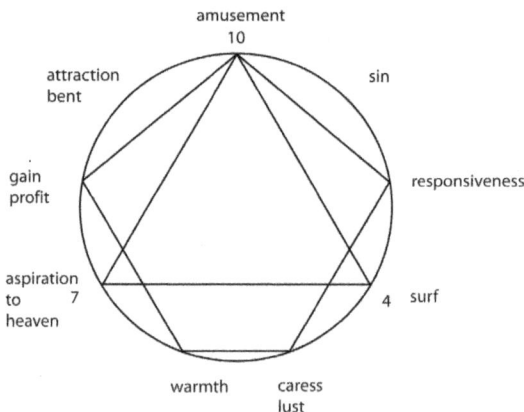

Amusement	unworthy qualities of man
Sin	unworthy manifestation of psychical-physical factor 2 result of "profit," growth of sinfulness as a result of the fall at the commitment of unworthy action
Responsiveness	outward action as a result of psychical-physical processes of inward reaction
Surf	blood
Caress, lust	result of unworthy manifestation of psychical-physical factor
Warmth	inward result as consequences of outward bent
Aspiration to heaven	higher parts in blood
Profit	rule about lack of fall lust to break proprieties and expenditures
Attraction	result of penetration of entry into "sphere" of another person as a consequence of outer pressure produced as a result of psychical-physical qualities

This is enneagram with «hidden» hexameter. The cycle of enn has entry at ten. When we speak of functional processes, there is an entry at nine and exit the same place so that there are ten stages, and nine holds proceeding together. When it is pentagramic enneagram, the idea is that here ten is at the beginning of pentagram, and ten is one order higher. The fact it can be at this place, the ten, is also because there might be another enneagram, hidden behind it, a functional one, with nine at this stage, so that two enneagrams belong to the same process and each stage at the same time corresponds to both of them, and would have both numbers. It might be more complete scheme. For this reason the periodic line here is given the same way, as it would be for traditional presentation, that is, it is symmetrical to central triangle. Sin 2 is the end of period.

Juliette Eden

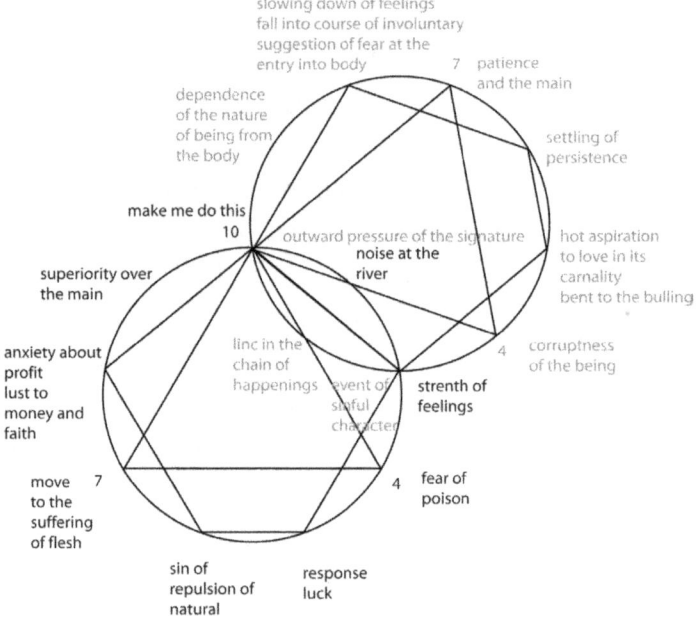

Enneagram of Impossibility to Exit a Situation

For the common enneagram:
10 – slowing down of lechery
2 – natural corruption of spirit

These two points create tension of an inward kind and impossibility to manifest under these conditions.

(Entry in between)

Third enneagram enters in between two at points 2 and 10, and then they coincide at 10 and 3. These stages are "swept" in between two schemes—reaction of victim goes into scheme of violator, and violent act into scheme of victim.

Story of Enneagram

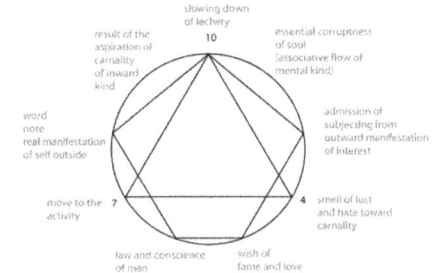

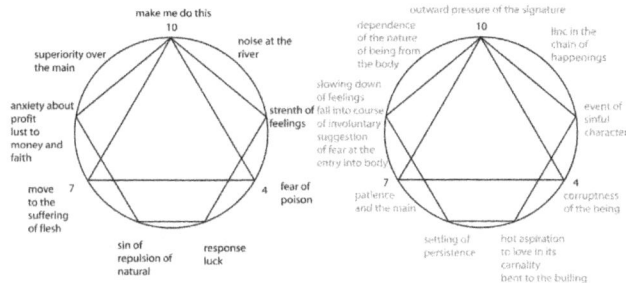

Violator

Make me do this
Noise at the pond
Strength of emotion
Fear of poison
Response, luck
Sin of repulsion of natural
Move to the suffering of flesh
Anxiety about profit, lust to money and faith
Superiority over the main

Victim

Outward pressure of signature
Link in the chain of events
Event of sinful character
Corruption of being

Fever, aspiration to love in its carnality, bent to bulling
Settling of persistence
Patience and the main
Slowing down of feelings, fall into course of involuntary suggestion of fear at the entry into body
Dependence of the nature of being upon the body

Through the 10 and 3

Common

1   slowing down of lechery
2   natural corruption of spirit (associative flow of intellectual kind)
3   acknowledgment of dependence from outward demonstration of interest
4   smell of lust, hate toward carnality
5   wish of fame and love
6   law and conscience of man
7   move to the activity
8   word, note, real manifestation of self outside
9   result of aspiration of carnality of inward kind

     2
8   reaction to violence
     5

2 – outward
5 – outside factor
8 – inward factor

2 violator   here it is and I want it
8 violator   that is if he wants, then it is permitted

Story of Enneagram

Reciprocity of victim and sinful lust

Common enneagram is a kind of reciprocal maintenance of worldly circ. It connects a cyclic process of a rapist with its significant victim, all three enneagrams or plans, moving through steps two and ten, even if they have different names for each of the schemes, it is the same position, only perceived from that perspective. Besides, stages ten and three are coming from another scheme for two nine-folded processes of rapist and its victim. This common enn connects them, then they coincide at three and ten — the thing is in sweep. It doesn't matter, if the rape happenes this is an approach toward it. Let us review steps of interpenetration. For common enn it is slowing down lechery (10) and the natural corruption of spirit (2), meaning — associative flow of the intellectual kind. For Violator, it is Make me do this (10) — taken out of a victim's reaction and noise at the river (2), meaning here it is and I should do something. At victim's scheme, there is Outward pressure of signature (10), taken from rapist's intentional plan, and Link in the chain of happenings (2), outward factor in a triad of victim's reaction toward the violent act. This way, we have interconnection of two steps with three factors, tenth step with factors of outward pressure of personality of insistent man, reactionary character of victim, and *slowing down of lechery*, meaning of total that enter like the facts of someone *not wishing* for a thing with active opposition. For the second pose, it is a strange aspiration toward an activity from some, position in the situation, and natural corruption of spirit, or mental associations about sexual drive.

Then schemes coincide at ten and three, with sweep in between factors from one scheme to another. In a victim's scheme there is an *event of sinful character*, meaning what used to be of unpleasant feature. At the third step of «violator» diagram is Strength of feelings. This intensifies the process. In victim's scheme, second and third positions are for spatial-temporal factors of what happened. Fifth and sixth stages are for intentional emotion, eight and nine for body performance. Those steps that go into a triangle also make for the scheme of situation-emotion-body, sequentially 10-4-7.

On the common scheme it is the situational nature of the community of the subject — it's leveled. One's attitude and subjects put along with the activity on the circumference. As an inner triangle relates to the common action, at fourth, there are two kinds of reactions; it is the nature of requirement of wrong stuff (smell of lust) and disgust of it from its possible victim's side. At seven, there is moving toward the activity. This way, opposition is hidden. It is passive. (slowing down of lechery). If we would look at stage four, it predisposes realization, which is expressed at stage three (admission of subjecting). At the same time, there is also pressure from natural impressions we have from childhood of «not being wrong,» etc., because of which we need to hold on, not to move, waiting for natural resolution of the problem (stage six). For the nine, it is also subjecting now from being under the influence of different low-standing tendencies, which we also might have, so that we react on such, produced by someone, and cannot occupy with other aspirations because love, which we have, also might have carnality in us, or we just have remnants of what we used to feel. Triad 2-5-8 is a material upon it works. Three stages coincide with 2 – intellect for function, 5 – sensitivity, 8 – emotional correction (conscience).

Upon victim's scheme, second and third stations are for intentional sensations, fifth and sixth for natural qualities, and eighth and ninth for intellectual emotion. The «coming» factor out of victim's scheme for the ten, this way corresponds to the common spread of factors; it is intentional sensation, and for the three. So, reason for the schemes to intercept and «exchange» their factors is because those factors correspond to the atmosphere and belonging of another scheme. However, the third situation is required for them to come into contact.

XXXXX

Priority to harm is psychological manifestation, even outward. If we know it, we partly are in a protective field because one might not get such person's intention. We need to decipher the outcome if we begin to investigate, but for this we need a hint or something to catch our attention. Otherwise, it is possible to know statements as they are, of what it is and its optional preview. Into what is of influence, it is the desire of its (influences) bearer to make up for the coming together of events, and then capture by surprise; this means that it is presupposed, we know nothing, or at least don't expect it in such value, and this is supposition. Its hidden character is concealing of pressure and possible future actions, all «building up» around the one being under target, and finding and fitting together all of what belongs, with the introduction into it having a different meaning than what it has from one's perspective. This has to do with Initiality of action, impossible considerations, exchange of values. Across the positions relating to an outward situation, there are physical factors — one is for the brain, misplaced feelings, reactions, up to paranoia — and another for substantial ones, or body pressure, as everything is imprinted. There are influences, they come and go, so factors are not always present, and this as well prevents us from seeing or making correct judgment, true issues, explanations, because we think it has passed away so it's not there. In reality, it is just put aside. Emotionally, all is explained for bearer of pressure through misgivings, personal adequacy, a lot of wording, corruption to which is given character of true purpose. Entry into participation, clear pressure, or transition to action—stage six. With possible cowardice (five), so it is the opposite.

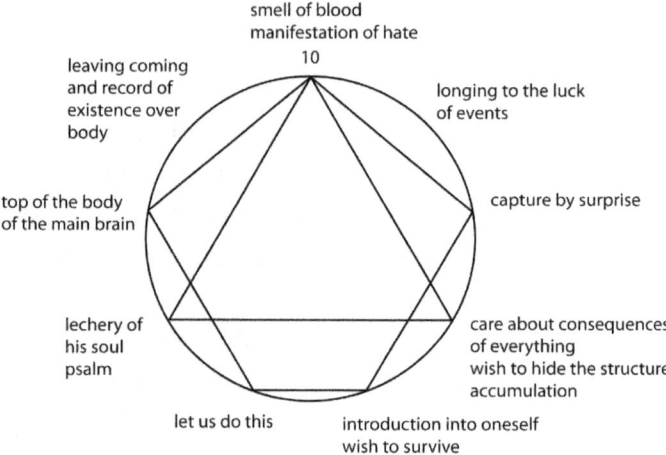

Enneagram of Move to Action

```
        2
8              function
        5


        9
3              intention
        6


        10
            ability to act
7       4
```

2, 3 – outward coming together of events
5, 6 – feeling
8, 9 – result

This is enneagram on the same theme as foregoing one, which differs by the fact that it is only one, no victim's reaction.

Enneagram of Physical Violence

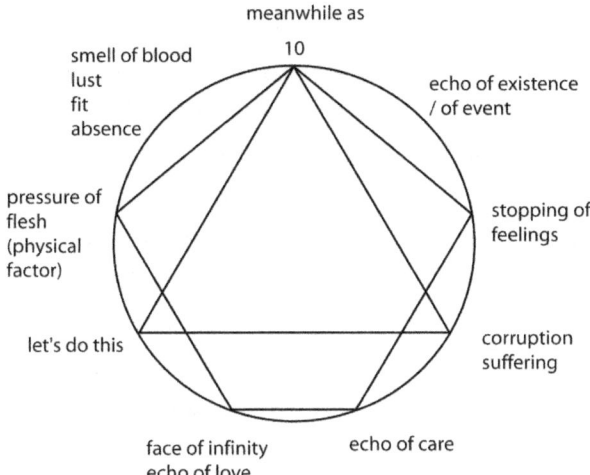

meanwhile as
smell of blood, lust, fit, absence
pressure of flesh (physical factor)
let's do this
face of infinity, echo of love
echo of care (pretence)
corruption, suffering
stoppage of emotions
echo of existence (of event)

meanwhile as—in the chain of events
corruption of lecher, suffering of victim
stoppage of feelings as a result of collision of sincere aspiration with a violent outward act

8 – physical violence
5 - pretence
2 – unfortunately, it happened

Into this enneagramatic requirements enter both act of pressure and victim's emotion. Knowledge of existence of violence means nothing in consistency of what one really feels in such happenings. For this reason we should not consider it to be too much in expression as stopping feelings of sixth and, partly, fourth stage. Subject, relating to the violent action, is at stages seven, five, also partly at fourth and eight. Ten is a chain of events and cannot not relate to both sides. Face of infinity, echo of love, at sixth stage is for our world in subsidence. At the moment one passes out, one is clean because of shock, and keeps clinging to what he used to be good in comparison with, for example, violence one experiences. One can believe it to be invariably good to make sure one is dead, after he is passing out, but in connection with stages nine and six, this gives a strange picture of the absence of compassion and consideration about possible punishment. My main feature, I do not want it. For the oppressor, it is a factor of annoyance, reason of doing it, all the spectacle of mockery over someone's possibility to suffer and impossibility finally to continue what he was doing very well without someone's help to spoil his future by this action.

Result of the Suffering of Victim

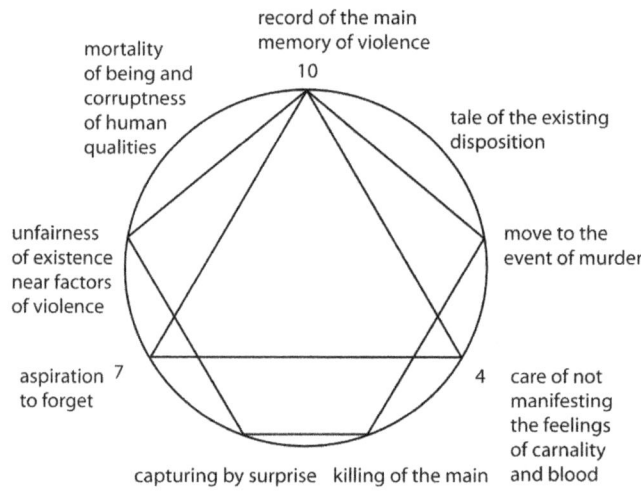

This is a very easy scheme, without much to explain. However, the subject is required to know. If we experienced something wrong, it gets imprinted in us. One can understand, it is unimportant to learn requirements of consideration — how and why. What is good is not of our capacity to know, but we can know if it is bad and all. We don't suppose there are harmful things till we meet them. When we meet them, we by no means should accord to the fact of appearance of wrong does it touch us or not, independent on how close it is. Still, I experience pressure from out of this. With consideration of placement for station, let us begin. This is *after* it happened. All this is for our inner quality of experience. There are different factors, some them relate to what happened and others to what one does. Sixth and fifth stages at the base of pentagram have to do with what is done for doing it and what is made during violent act. Killing of the main means there is a loss; without consideration and self-justification, we are done. Second and third stages are for inner world of the victim, return of cognition. One acquires ability to judge and checks the world around. Then, he recalls the event. Third stage is the place of interval, something should've happen, or doesn't happen. Coming from preceding stage two, one aspires to forget, but as one can't, one moves to impossibility to agree to the fact of continuation of experience, and not just being done with existence. The totality of the process is manifested in the fact that we are not invulnerable; there are issues concerning our instability and there is no need to define them. Simpler, something *could* be done, for escape. We are touched and don't want to be dirtied (4). As final destruction comes, there remains the record of the main and the memory of violence.

Section Three

Enneagrams of Human Problematic

Enneagram of Poetic Gift

Here, all the pairs are done in opposition of forces, leading to perseverance of position, each of it. This way, it is both sides of the compass, and nothing at all. Fruit of the work and the beginning of it. Timeless and current. Currency of time and start of proceeding. Mind and soul. Hard work and inspiration. Congratulation and absence of capability. Etc.

2 and 3 is for function
5 and 6 is for human being
8 and 9 is for spiritual reactivity

The top of pentagram is for dimensions of time and space (up and down, right and left, none, epochs and epos).

A periodic line 1-4-2-8-5-7 let us see our move from whatever toward the running start somewhere at this time. This way one enters into eternal; into epochal quality and permanence of temporal. Then the fruit comes, but here it is marked together with desire to create, so it is process in its activity.

Then it is resultant upon us and the world; we carry this cross of being renown, while it spreads. Then it is understanding and realization of what it is, but also happiness. Then it is recognition, but we aren't able any longer. And we go back to the initial point in nowhere and anywhere.

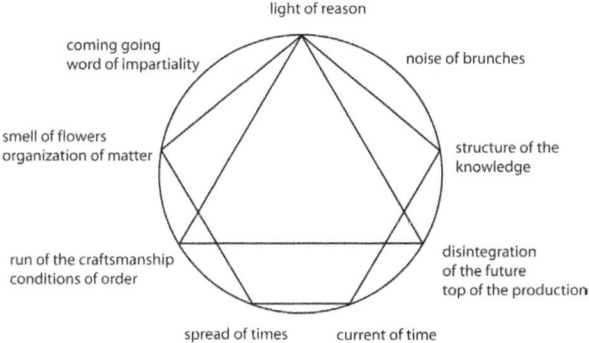

Enneagram of the Memory of Past

Everything leaves a memory after itself. It is not that we just remember. The scheme includes not only a memory but also a material for it. What we remember has material existence. It is also placed in time. There are as well key to the knowledge, our ability to remember, what carries such function, etc. It's hard to tell what is worth remembering and what isn't. This way we talk in general of just what is possible to remember. There is also the question of: is it possible to remember what we never saw, because everything is gone before we are. Therefore, we cannot acknowledge that here we are in the empty space, there is no past, etc. People talk about consequences as a time machine question. However, changing the past from *here* is probably impossible. Still, idea of changing the past, or predicting the future, is always here because we wish it. This way, cause is important as long as it is sequential. The thing about memory is that to try and change it, one definitely has to accept the idea of the *existence* of real factors—not just delusion—or there is nothing to talk about if nothing does matter. For example, if there is something out of nowhere, it is at its placement in time and impossible to talk of it as just a possible situation-anywhere. From another side, if events have common nature, there would be similarity. This should be separated to see the specialty of *this* very case from general factors; for example, disappearance of species in the process of planetary evolvement. So, what enters into the *memory of the past* is about everything relating to considerations of info, materiality, and even energetic questions. There is no separation, however, of these parts. For example, light of reason, at tenth, is a fine matter with properties. There is an indicator of inclination toward this or that side. At the base of pentagram, the spread of times relates to all pieces or lands of subscribal. The current of time is transition in time at one of these spreads. What is at the base of the triangle speaks about certain mentation toward sub-creation (production, top of it; run of craftsmanship). Then, at intervals, there are what has relation to how the world is constructed; is it more of information, or materiality? What could be taken that has its roots of materiality is more important in construction than knowledge. From certain sides, it's easy to construct the system where knowledge could flow, but to organize the matter with the same properties, esthetic and meaning, never can be accomplished. For this reason there is Smell of Flowers; because there is tuning, it is the atmosphere of what is important. Back to the triangle, craftsmanship exists for doing things better, so it is the *top* of the production. The most *difficult* points of enneagram, connected with 10, are at the second stage; being a slowing down factor is our responsibility or mindset. Coming out toward hearing. The inner octave would include transforming powers, the ability to hear, transportation through the air, meaning, deciphering, etc. From the opposite factor of slowing, it is another side of it; it is coming, going, and word of impartiality, which presupposes that there is at least no lie. At ten there comes what traveled all the way of circumference. We cannot tell it's maya, meaning the whole world is just my reason and only through our perception world exists. Or that if we won't have perception nothings would matters. There might be someone else perception. It is just a scheme of how one remembers. So, I'm using the scheme, maybe relating to other thing(s), but corresponding to the flow of process in this case also, so that it might be applied.

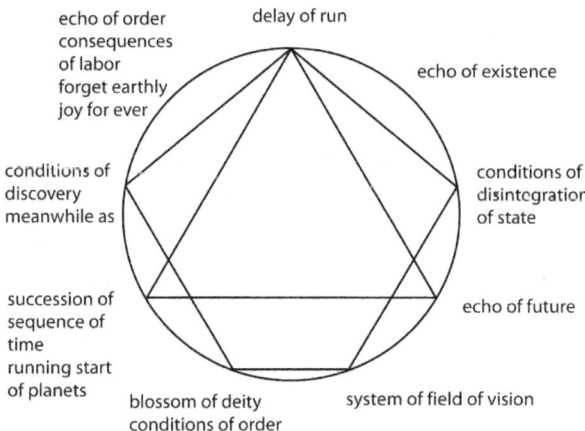

Enneagram of the Flow of Utility

1 step and step—10 —delay of run (together) then; steps are toward the direction of fixation
2 what our daily life is like
3 forces of decay of any conditions
4 next period of life that is in the future but would have the same set without a changes

5 viewing, plan, in common, general featuring points in spreads of slices
6 how it flows, current of leading life like this with its pleasures and mechanical running
7 what is of higher points that touch us, not quite out of the scheme, just upon this level
8 flowing of timing, and possible new additions
9 stabilized condition of life and how it makes us feel unhappy because of its enclosure

Life triangle	3	6	9
Problematic	4	7	10
Reconsideration	2	5	8

Process viewed from the side of the periodic line (1-4-2-8-5-7) gives it from perspective of a story-like sentence. Steps made toward fixation for better comfort, appreciating it to be going in the same set in the future, for the sake of daily living, with possible conditions of additional accommodations, linked with what is maintained already in general, taking into consideration possible existence of wishes, and admirations for better fixation. This is if we would count a step one also, as a first one, and the last comes upon a tenth.

life of being
2 life in general of each day   3 inescapable running down

life of reaction
5 all together, sphere and overview   6 reaction upon usual

life of situation
8 how it would continue to work in   9 running out of order
the future

Enneagram of Waste of Conscience and Echo

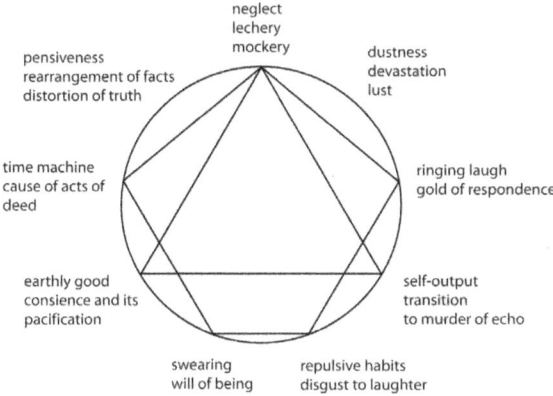

Particular enneagram with psychological application on the fact of existence of corruption. It is permeated by idea there is spending or loss of energetical field. This field is there for human qualities. Conscience and response are coming out of this field. Here is the process where this is lost. How does it happen? We need to react in a particular way; this way there is ignorance of these things at point ten. Out of it is physical reaction, reaction on a physical level, because of the leading, initial signal to pass this. Ten is reaction, two is spatial. Concentrated powers bring up a third stage — now it is self-elevation, putting oneself into position of only importance. This brings again the question of will; as it cannot coexist on this plane just like this, there should be application. This is self-output and the move toward the deadening of any vibration. This permits the stabilization of how it is from the outside and the intention inwardly. Then it is about bigger and bigger will power; however, it cannot embrace any *big* area due to its qualities. It is squirming of fits. Life, its flow, has its requirements and demands. This way, we come to the next point of the base of triangle; it is acquisition and pacification of conscience. The eight stage is nucleus. It talks of the fact, things remain the same. There where no reevaluation. Even if what was done is removed back over the time, it doesn't become insignificant. There is new setting, but there is the same feeling of guilt. This strange thing, having to cover oneself up now re-judges the whole totality of factors; it is the rearrangement of dry facts, with ignorance of true placement, not to notice meaning, because then one would blame oneself, so that it is the distortion of truth.

Enneagram of Corruption of Being

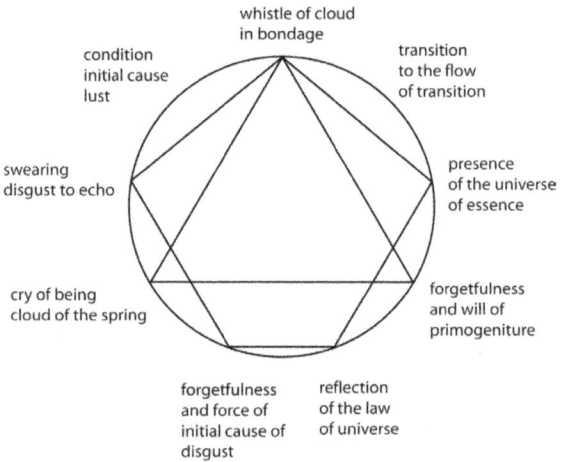

Corruption of being is corruption of being. All the stations are part of the process. Second stage is for removal into the sphere of run. For example, one becomes involved. It has around an atmosphere of absence and somnolence. There is the subtle feeling of move. One as if agrees to be pulled into this flow. So, it's not quite involuntary. There is the premonition of something being ahead, some action to take place, not just a movement. Third is the feeling in us, response, on what has been put into us, hereditary, with the birth as homo sapience. Like a cloud of "common" stuffing used for this purpose, it is the feeling of connection with it. As being born, man feels the right to be angry. He forgets it is for another purpose and uses his ability of self-will for wrong. It is the fourth stage. Fifth is for us being an apparatus reflector of natural processes; alas, there is no self-will. Action on a low level of trans-substantiality is predefined.

Six — one forgets he's a human being, not only a body, and feels disgust for nature. Inside of it, there remain feelings needed for other purposes; now they give a stirring feeling of craving and anticipation of "youthfulness" and mortality — the seventh. At eight, its stage is now to hate any outcome of vibratory nature upon us, whenever there is involved something not of the body but of feelings. Then comes the final stage of reaching up to consciousness, and there is only corruption. It happened before we started, initiating a total process. Ten is just a noise of not being born correctly. There are higher powers, and they have been subsided into a strange act of disappearance of totality of what makes one a part of humanity.

Period. 10 to 4: accumulation of wrong stuff; 4 to 2: giving up; 2 to 8: disappearance of any protective measure; 8 to 5: decision to be as bad as one could be in the body.

Section Four

Enneagram on how Essence of Earthly Interest makes Reflections

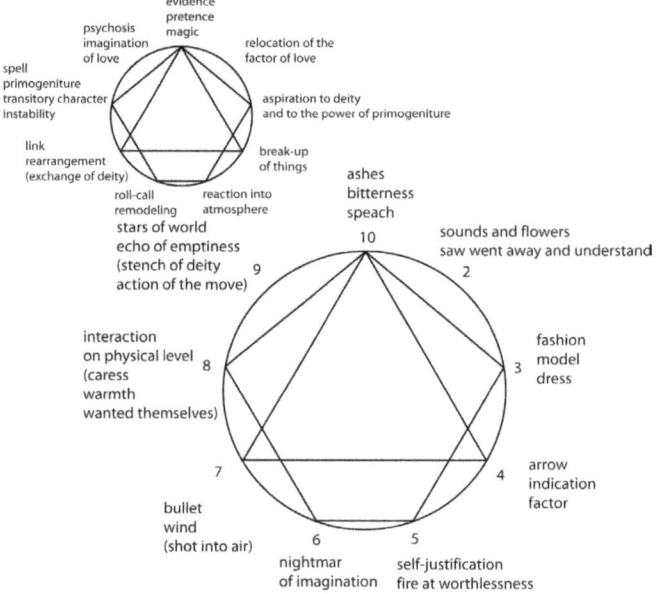

I'm going to give an enneagram with one of the steps fully explained in terms of inward co-response of stages. The title presupposes that here it is taken as an example process of coordination of reactions and attribution of what one wants to banal and functional features. This way, enn is an image of this schematic output of totality of what governs all of it. I will begin from the explanation of inward octaves of one of the stages, the ninth. These stages are put into a small enneagram upon the scheme. Factors go in pairs along a vertical top factor. From 2 to 9:

2 exchange of love of wish	9 invention on its base (of love attachment)
3 ability to feel the will power	8 inclination to slip down and weakness
4 absence of coherency/meaning	7 connection and giving up to this fact (of 4)
5 what is proceeding has reflexion	6 gathering, taking into account, parody

In this way, what is on the left side of enneagram makes up for what is on the right. There is a meaning behind this connection — if we look for another subject to love it, and there is a psychic instability and ill imagination, it is probably evoked (both factors) by the fact that the subject doesn't correspond to true possible feelings; this is why there is instability. If we have a will and yet we slip down to weakness, look for imaginary possibilities, it means direction of intention does not answer the real factor either. There is an absence of coherence, and, henceforth, it is required to link and bind and rearrange things together again. Then it is reaction, and the overview again of all things, and making another model. Three factors at ten correspond to three powers — equal but differing in nature (please look at the scheme). This way, this small enneagram is all about absence of true subject of attention. It cannot answer the reasons for why it is happening; it reflects how this relates to the same factuality. All this relates to number nine of big enn, whose title may explain that it is about acting, initiated by a feeling of eternity and also already corrupted religiously or higher inspirational stuff.

Triangle 2-5-8 of big enn is 2 for emotional, 8 for physical, and 5 for intellectual. Another triangle 3-6-9 is 3 for physical, 9 for emotional, and 6 for intelect. It is a particular system of interactive activity. So, 4 is for next decisional making, three is a model — an example of how things should be. Five, six, and ten are negative factors, because they stumble upon the process, and seven is reaction, with eight as a habit — also possibly a fast decision. Nine is also inconsistency. Negative factors are conditioned by the fact that earthly interests always bring disillusion. At the same time it includes function 3 and 4 for well-working and successful results.

Enneagram of Lechery and Light (Power of Knowledge of Earthly Fact [Factor])

The next enneagram has examples for inner octaves of second and seventh stages. First, let's take examples of totality of action, then after a discussion of inward octaves see it in detail. The bigger enneagram and its title are example of someone's character. Here it is person with developed psychic abilities, who has a knowledge. He strives up, but is compiled to occupy in his life with interactions upon the low level. To do so is a corruption. Factors belong to totality of process; inclusion is for those that answer the factors, predisposed in the title. The scheme should work in its interactions, so that if there is a mistake, it should be obvious. The main factor, which skips the idea of belonging to truth, sets up totality of process (10). Without it, this would not have a place. However, behind it there should be small steps of forgetfulness (of how true things affect and respond to it), so that it would be missed. This also involves a sensational feeling, because truth makes us change, or its absence does. Because of this, nine is the misleading feeling not to notice this. Our intellect reacts; this gives us the eighth step of consideration about totality of existence, its reasons and source, etc., with falsity in it, because the true fact is already misplaced. However, life is going on and it is all right, so that one can exist, and even wonderfully, under these conditions (7). At the same time, all suppressed factors exist side by side with sensations and wishes, and under these circumstances it gives rise to all kinds of corrupted feelings and actions, as the following (6).

Story of Enneagram

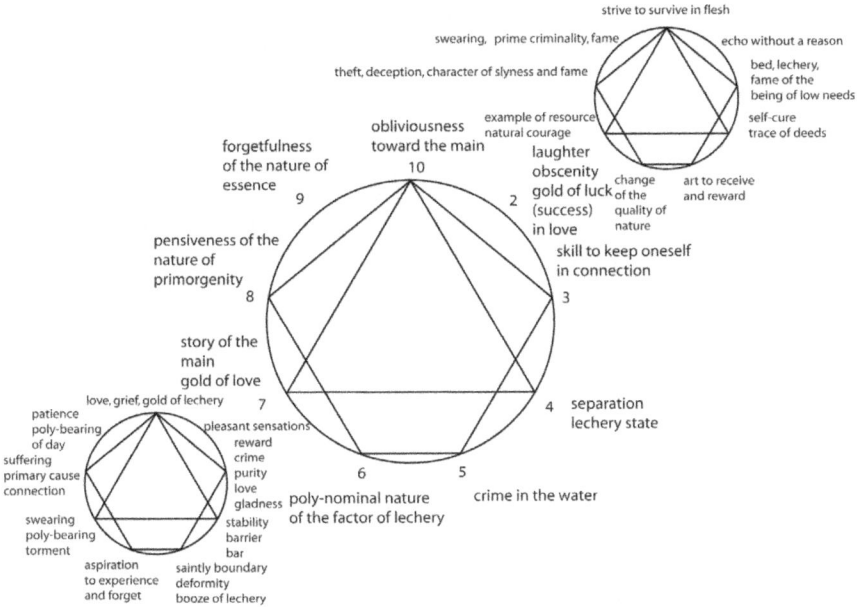

This brings to this or that kind of wrongdoing (5). The factor of truth was absent from the beginning, so that reality of this fact of doing wrong cannot be taken as one; for this reason there comes separation, not to notice, and at the same time the state continues (4). One has to get out, but the third station is an ability to find one's way, or informationary questioning. Man's persona is qualified and developed; therefore, there is a compilation of these qualities at the second stage. This way, six is a passive factor, five is an action, four is consciousness, three is functional intellectual ability, two is essence of man. Seven is connection with life around, eight is intellectual association, nine is spiritual avoidance from the side of essential, and ten is the same, only from an intellectual side. So, they go like this in pairs: 2 and 9 for essence, 3 and 8 for intellectual functional. Ten is connected with one (first steps); this is why there are no arrows to and out of the tenth stage on the schematic diagrams where there is an exchange of qualities.

If to take inner octaves, even though a separated unit, they have to correspond to the station in making up its qualities. This way, station two, man's essence — here corresponding to the theme of schematic psychological and physiology as well — is a compilation of what makes up this stage's feature of attitude and character. Taken in close example, it could be put into the enneagramatic scheme also. This way, art to receive and reward (5) answers to the fact of successful love interactions, as well as the third stage (bed, lechery, being of low necessities) speaks about the lecherous position of sexual habits. When we look at this smaller diagram, it corresponds with its stages to the bigger one, to which it belongs. We take as a character a developed personality of man. Also, inclinations, so that stages speak of process in hand, and its nature. All is taken in its static, with points in interaction. For ten of the small enneagram it is strive to survive in flesh. This corresponds to the theme of primary enneagram. There is a power of knowledge of earthly factor. So, one tries to preserve in a flesh, having a necessity of survival. At the same time he wishes to keep his own essence. Considering the name of the second stage we see here already a predisposed idea. On top of the scheme, at the second and ninth steps, there are factors answering the response. It is (at two) a natural quality of answering and reacting upon things not necessarily in demand, and at nine its corresponding stage of saying too much, falsification, stories. The top corners of pentagram, places of interval, are for the activity outside, with inner qualification; it could be called passive for three, as a requirement, and active for eight, as some kind of expression outside of man. Stages at the base of the triangle, as their counterpart at ten, are more toward whole nature and totality. Because this three compose together a basic frame. These are consequences (trace of deeds), and fixation (self-cure) for the fourth stage. And also, natural courage to do this, and resources, for the seventh. Lower corners of the pentagram stand for artificial qualities with qualification.

The observation of the nine stages for the seventh stage of bigger enneagram is as following. It consists of contradiction and survival of tension. At its tenth stage there are three factors. These are like three powers, with different nature. One, another that opposes it, and third that is an exit out of it. It is expressed as love, grief, and ability to move into lecherous sphere, to survive it. Accordingly, at the points of slowing down, the situation and collision of development, two and nine, it is pleasant sensations, which agree in nature to the idea of process, and its opposing factor is what brings or is of necessity to survive the day, usual routine, as it is perceived by decent chap. Point eight of the interval here is very meaningful in terms of its context, of suffering, in connection with the fact that there is primary cause, makes it significant, as well as a connection. This way it bears participation, not just passively. Interval at three bears a lot of wording, different in nature; it is in a way in opposition of the eighth stage in terms of absence of suffering, as there is reward, crime, purity, and love at the same time. This might work for the fact that there is a separation from feelings; it is expressed at point four as stability, bar, barrier. From another side, it is particular numbness of feelings at stage seven. Behind it, there exist those feelings that relate to high up in their substitution—both sanctity and deformation, with deception of delusionary powers, and aspiration of experience once and again.

Enneagram of Corruption of Data and Lechery of Low Source

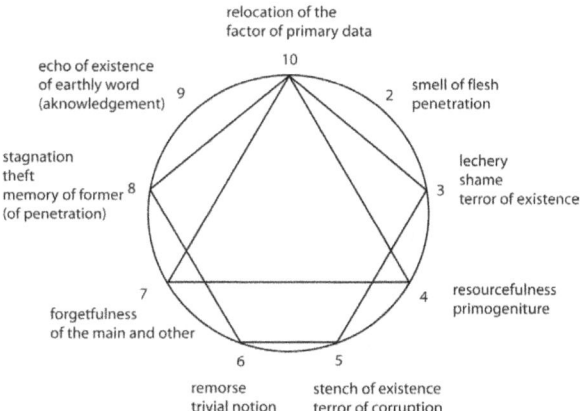

This is an example of screwed up yet conscious behavior of someone not wishing the true data become available. This way, there is an exchange of real facts; real fact is displaced into another setting so that it doesn't have a correct meaning anymore. All other stations relate to the psychic attitude of persons leading this process. All this is one leveled features of psychic qualification. The triangle, not entering into a period, is a common attitude toward life's reality. It is acknowledgement of the fact that it is present the way it is. It is as well just one's own dirtied everything. Triad 2-5-8 relates to the process of living. Two is what is being done; five is what atmosphere is around corrupted actions, and it is also fright that these actions would be uncovered. At eight transaction is subsided. There is stagnation. It is result of repeated corrupted actions. To the fact of relocation of data there are also added the put down reality of truth (7), and also the ability to dip into reservoir of emotional and intellectual belonging.

Enneagram of Primordial Beginning

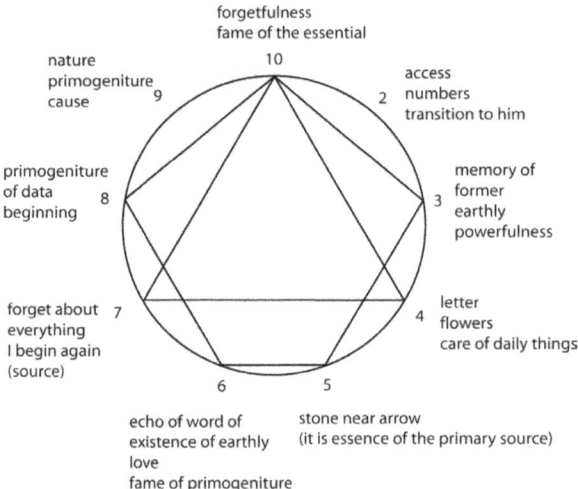

Here is an abstract idea of initial cause. Factors that enter into this process could be described in general terms as necessity to the totality of its fact. Whole (9) is a source itself. Ten is repetition. There is also a point of start (eight). And repetition of beginning again and again. The sensual factor is six. The material factuality of begin (five). Proceeding (4). Past currency (3). Digital account (2). This way, fourth stage is present, and third is past. Seven is a recurrence. Six is reaction. Two is mental. Ten is requirement of life, and it is important, as a next level (two digits), which is on top of everything; it means that we forget and live it through again, having all the feelings and sensations of the moment. Then it is cause (9), point of start (8), and materiality of it (5). If it would be one, it is an entity. If to observe periodic line, for example, if we really have a primordial existence but forget it getting born into present (ten to four). Then we acquire the mental ability, as a child, we learn how to count, and think (four to two). Two to eight, which is called the beginning, means, we recall. We begin to ponder things over. From there we go to sensations (eight to five). That is, begin to live in a body again. And we begin again, anew, each of the things, and forget it (seven to ten), for the sake of present (ten to four).

We have essence (10) so we begin again (7) and come into the present (4). Data has its personal beginning; there is the source (5) and it transits (2) as long as it comes from somewhere. So that 10, 7, and 4 is the world, and 8, 5, 2 is an essence. 9, 6, 3 is the background. It is the background of existence.

Enneagram of Corruption of Flesh and Spiritual Connection of a Human

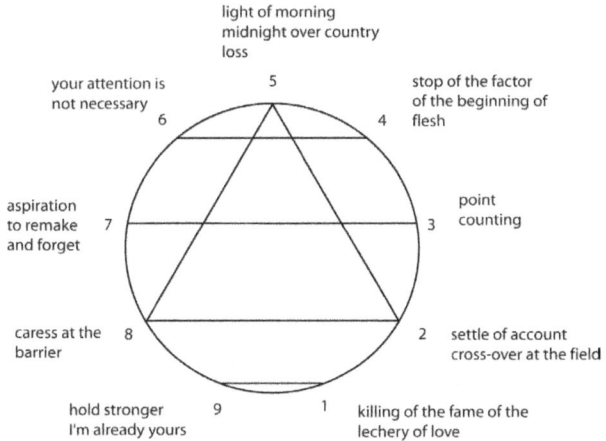

Juliette Eden

This is the transcription of the situation when man is enclosed for some reason into the inability to reach high. He can see things from another side. We see here turned over enneagram where on top is five. For this reason, instead of ten we put one, because it is below. Relocated primary factors remain the same; what is wrong is position. Here 2 and 3 are for possible intellectual reconsideration, 8 and 9 for sensual feelings and aspiration, but 6 and 5 are for failure. Here are clear the stages of triad 1-4-7; it is the intention for 1, wish for 7, and self-determination not to do much with one's body.

Position of enneagram makes sense in terms of transcription of process. Its name let us understand that we view this from the side of materiality; however, all other factors remain as spiritual necessity. This way, there is a double process of aspiration and survival.

From the top of enn, where it is a loss, this speaks of a potential story behind; there is already a lot (light of morning, midnight over country). It is already about overcoming, distribution, accord, and discordance. Six and four follow the process in gradation. 6 is outside factor, and 4 is decision at this time. Seven and three are therefore renewal, but upon the ground of former attachment. Then, it is separation. (Account is closed.) We go. It is a continuation up to anything (at the bar). Nine means we reached and entered, and have response. What former problem there used to be, of substitution, is no longer there (stage number one).

1, 5, 6   Situation
7, 8, 9   Wish
4, 3, 2   Desire

Enneagram of Reflection (Representation) of Love

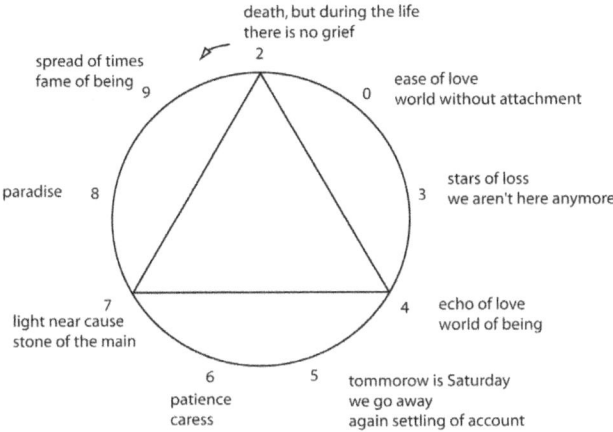

This scheme with an exchange of factors (figure two is placed at the tenth stage, and on its place there is zero) tells of enneagramatic qualities where there is a broken sequence, but still it is harmonized in its connections. Arrow means transition of what should be at second stage back, and on its place appears an empty space or opening. What should be at the tenth stage disappears; this way all stages are already exchanged in their features to make up for new schematic interrelations.

7, 4, 2	triad of fire
9, 6, 3	earth and sky
8, 5, 0	heaven

The exchange of pattern happens under pressure. But, man retains one's qualities. However, something goes away, and photo is different. As sky manifests upon earth, it is therefore a triad of earth. It is fire, earth, and heaven; water is everywhere.

Enneagram of Corruption of Creative Life and Spiritual Flight

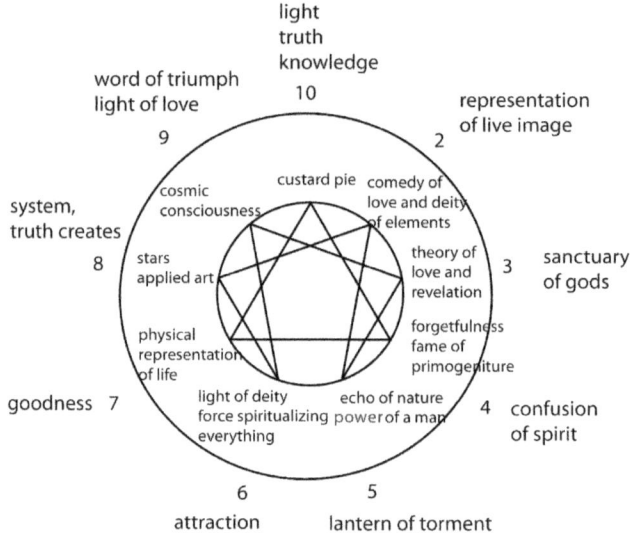

5 is lantern of torment — nightmare of love and ghost of deity

We have in us the possibility to accept higher influences. This is the meaning of spiritual flight, which existence might be escaped but also incorporated into one's life. What is important for creativity is that it (of spiritual) should enter into our creation as existential and spiritual requirements, if we have understanding of such. However, creativity often gets corrupted because we have pressure upon us from social and living requirements. Here, it is a sequence of stations, without a period, together with functional application. It is two schemes of one and the same upon different levels, or of a different kind. Reasons of corruption are not discussed. We see the process when it is already corrupted. The combination of a twofold nature of process is very intricate. It is not two sides but should be connected; subject should be approached from this perspective. Behind the meaning stated by the title of each stage of existential pentagramic enneagram, there is another one, applied to the functional. This presents the realization of the fact that spiritual flight *always* involves corruption of creative life.

Enneagram of Inability to Create a Living I

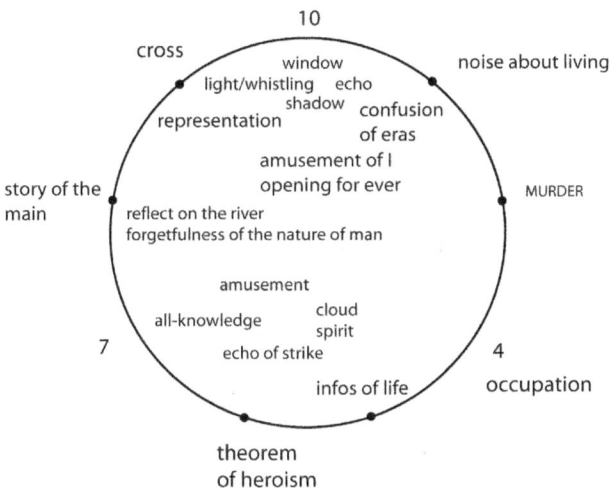

This is a schematic explanation of how it is wrong to try to create a living creature out of matter, without spiritual parts in it. However, the process is possible. We discuss not this process itself but reactions of people who do it. Upon the scheme, I put some parts of the process inside the circle, and some outside. It has to do with the specialty factor. In terms of placement, there are three stages that are considered outward — third, fourth, and sixth; and those that are inward — fifth, seventh, and tenth. The other three factors have their feature being of both kinds. These are second, ninth, and eighth. There is a difference in how we see each stage. Stage six is going to be explained further on as single enneagram. The idea of there being few sentences inside the circle for some of the stages is that there are few counterparts of each stage.

Four different meanings for the ten are easy to explain as light and whistling being our perception; this way, it is a window through which it comes, light which gives shadow and echo, a response to sound. Cross is our representation—again it is four sides. Reflexion (eight)—this way, these three stages 10, 9, and 8 fall into one group. Seven and six relate to outward participation in feelings. This way it speaks of inadequacy, the reaction and longing to forget. Infos of life and occupation are the same thing for the outward behavior. This way, the last two stages — noise of living and murder. A periodical line would give the process of someone's reaction on representation — an important feature of occupation — carrying the position at which it is possible, then a situational factor of dispersion of really important, meaningful longing into something inadequately corrupting; therefore, why is it picked up?

The explanation that it is not required but is popular is not enough. We don't know. At stage eight is the explanation why someone would be occupied with this trial, or take upon oneself. We have in us reflections of world outside. And here one also forgets the nature of man. This way the process is initiated. That's why it is the story of the main. Then, it is the gathering of information (5). Then again, it is amusement, drawing in this atmosphere of confusion, naturally taken hate and self-evolvement (all-knowledge). Back to representation means as an end and return to oneself, not withstanding an impossible act of corruption, but it also speaks of possible continuation. Again, this way we can see there was no entry into another, whatever was produced; it doesn't lead anywhere, but the source is clean. So, we can see a period also, but it is immersed into the scheme upon a different level. We cannot see the period if we take each subject in its features of what it really is; it is all mixture.

We cannot drop the quality of our being and word not necessary for egoistic expenditure, maybe, but we personally cannot.

Theorem, or something unimportant to find resolving to, on the act of heroic action. For some of the stages there are few definitions. Arrow means intentional move, indication of significance. Archer, I made my song — this is done, and I am this. Third stage is for particular atmosphere. We acted, but there is no one for us to applaud. It is also the feeling of absence and awaiting for someone to come, while we feel this like a fire. The very significance of action is at the fourth station, with the meaning that it used to be a mistake to do this; one has to suffer proper punishment, and one *might* count it clean. The fifth stage is just for explanation of placement in the four-dimensional world of spatial and time. Six here is for positive, which means the force of opposition of the world. Seven is another kind of response, or reactive, this time from human society. At eight it is for the idea of there being a transformation — if there is no me and I am asleep. Why is it involved, because now it is personal reaction. Nine — it is now separation. Here I am, here is the doer, and out of it comes the decision.

Theorem of Heroic Action

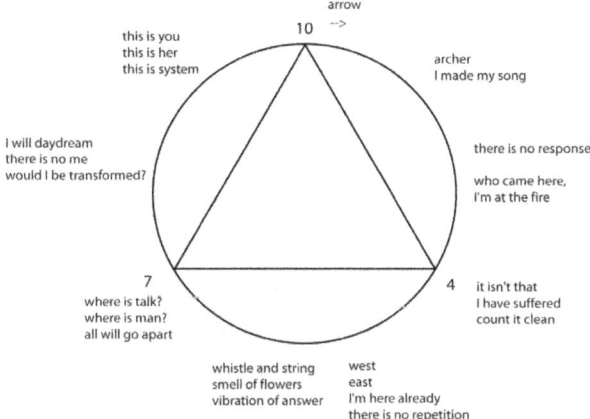

Enneagram of Fear and Despair

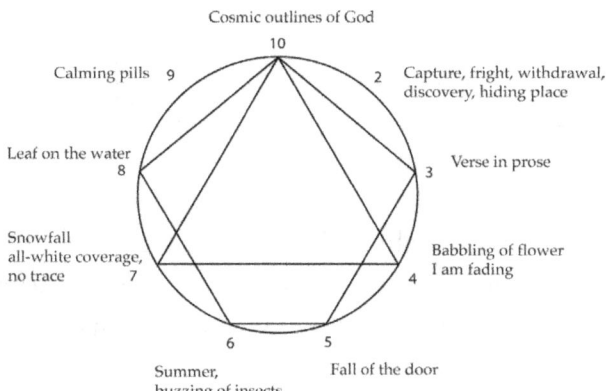

Whatever there is, it is a single process, if it is put into enneagram. All stages should correspond to it, this way or that way. Name given to the process should approach the reality of it. Let's take the problematic example of aging, and without defense or protection of real having *fear and despair.* Into considerations enter inclinations of character, which also might be in close proximity to universal, in the nature, but special for one. Because of it, it is more useful to look for placement of qualities, not qualities itself. The second stage is a compilation of situations and what makes it so (some obstacle). The third is something of outside, acquired and used, an adaptation. Fourth, in a way, is change, and change cannot go on forever. Five was told to be a novelty. But what enters into it comes out of preceding factors. Its meaning should be taken in connection with what there was at previous stages. This way, something is revealed (5). Six is transitory character; here it is continuation, but with decline. Here it is a desire not to have any production (seventh). At eight, where there is a gathering of crops, it is a fallen leaf, running not on current, just fallen. Totality (nine) is desire to calm oneself, even if by artificial means it happens. Ten, the source, here it is half-conscious appreciation of much higher things, but as long as they touch, the way one is. There is no action, except retrieval, also contemplative nature of perceptions (6).

One might not always be able to pose questions of profound nature. Why we had our life? What were we doing? It is not necessary important for those who are around us. This is as painful as anything. One looks for hiding place, to occupy with recollections. We recall the trifles. It is no longer possible to understand this is us who did it. Feel it again. Be happy that this were us. We don't want to remember, we look for calamity. With the flow of waters, time runs into its full reservoir and we are in. What was important? Life is gone, there is no one to understand our realm. We can make a pose, a verse in prose, one can see. But, it is the fall of the door—now not separated; we are only left with the image or feeling of God being enthroned. We understand.

Theorem of Ignorance of the Main I

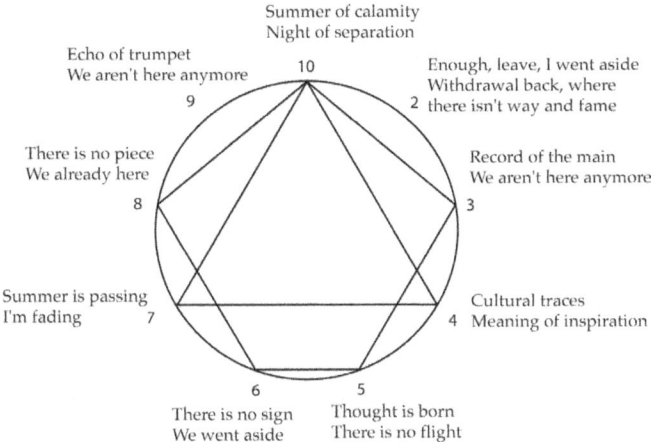

Our main I is what is of importance toward individuality. We can ignore it. However, the process involves those very factors we ignore. It is also supposition. We move around and continue to ignore it, but the very move is toward it. We might not suppose we immediately recognize what is the main. This way, we are coming toward this realization and understanding of factors of its main features.

The difference in between of what is at second and fourth stage is that second is for our inward world, and fourth is for world outside. To experience while we are amid our inner world, we are stepping aside. This way we gather our attention on what we are interested, to discuss it, make judgments, experience because it's not just mental phenomenon. It doesn't mean it is inactive, but we stay where we are. There is no way and no interaction outside; it is enough. Fourth is for experience the world around, but by location, with a choice. We are interested in something, and participate. Five is fixation. In a way it's low; it is the condition of development, but we know it's true. We come and go at two, and we travel at four; five is a home.

Nine is a strange thing, slogan used for it; it is for our option of not being here. We cannot manage; it has its features, as in three, where it is all wrong. But there are laws. Each step speaks of something we don't understand, what we didn't see, but we can feel it though. This is difficult for continuation. Six, where we are aside, means we have attention, but still we are not necessarily in control. This way, it is control at three, otherwise it would be impossible there, where all is wrong. Nine is clear, but we can stuck. Autumn, number seven, it is a world of its own. We can enter, but it disappears.

At eight, we are already here and there is work. Ten is above and not required, this way it is separated; it is not travel, not coming and going, not presence (6). We talk of materiality, discussing the subject. If to take the stages in terms of psychological application, the difference in features would be dramatic. This way we talk of application of scheme to a common factor, upon multiple levels of meaning. Info is not a main, it is our way, how we see it.

Section Five

Enneagram of Love and Sexual Intercourse

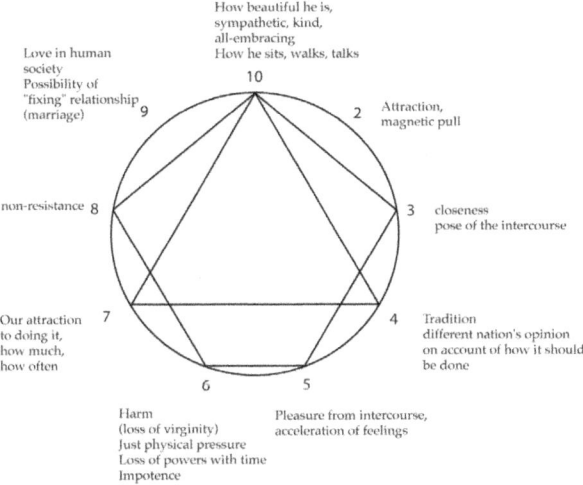

Here is the phenomenon of attachment in love. Into phenomenal enneagram enter mixed conceptions. It is possible to see in such kind of enn an opposition, a contrary subject — for example, how ugly man seems (10), or a pressure to make one bed (8) instead of agreement; repulsion instead of attraction, etc. At 7 it is cyclic. 9 is a human factor. At 2 enters what is usual for this. The third stage is what was particularly applied at this very case. Fourth is for how it could be done here and there. Fifth is an improvement, or what it is about it that might make it better. Six is always some kind of running out, deterioration. Eight is communication, even though here it is not quite clear, still it is about some kind of agreement, or conscious decision, led by wish, to be involved. This way, at such scheme, there is no exchange of qualities in between stages; they present themselves the way they are. Period is very clear. We see the man (or woman), which we like, immediately in our brain we have this idea of how it should be done in agreement with our society's overlook. This part goes first, then, when it is all right, we permit ourselves to be attracted. Henceforth, we don't resist. Then goes what it is done for, or a pleasure, running high on it, then it is a question of how often should we require this, and again return to the fact of how likable is a person. What doesn't enter in period is actually the way it is done (3), possible change, decline of feelings, powers (6), and a fixation of relationship, like a marriage or communal living.

Enneagram of Transformation of Soul into Nullity

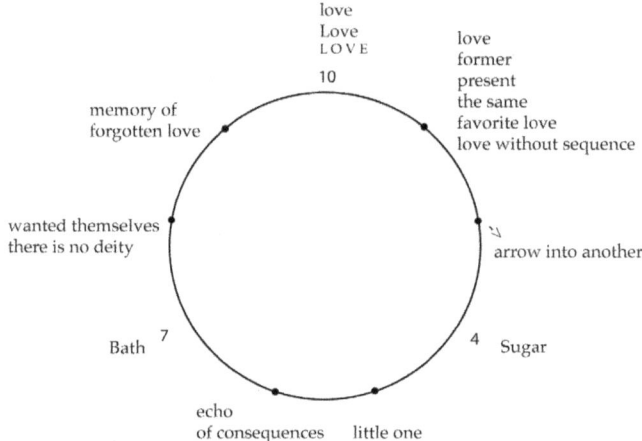

Here are three enneagrams to one and the same subject. This is a deterioration of a situation. First, enneagram of sequential quality speaks about the subject raised under circumstances or behavior (acting) in daily life. Second is psychological application in general terms (how we behave when we are pressed by all of life's surrounding.) Third is a common feature of any love in deterioration; it is mostly for the physical body, with its consequences (that is, we need to have relationships, even if we are incapable of the reality of feelings.) The

Story of Enneagram

initial setting predisposes to next the decline of personal attitude. It is as if we would be upon the hill, and it is necessary rolling down to stop at the plane below. This way, it is on top, rolling down, and coming to the halt. Ten. Three words for love signify love with all meanings we might attach. Love from a capital letter, and love as a symbol. Two. All kinds of love there might be. Three is for the change. Four is indispensable inescapable pleasure of any love interactions. Five is the feeling of intimacy, put into words or manifestation. Six is what proceeds out of all our actions in terms of subject. Seven is inescapable necessity to renew oneself. Eight is psychological instability; it is self-justification of one's worthiness, or trial to explain by other people's actions, or admittance of the absence of meaning in everything after the action is done. This way, on the right-hand side is the action, and on the left it is what comes out of it. Nine is a nonexistent requirement to remember what is already gone. By the circumference, it works with the idea of entry at the third station, experience and reaction (four and five), then reaction of the world upon us, hope of renewal, explanation and justification, and lost memory. Then at ten there is the abstract idea of love, and two is for what is on practice.

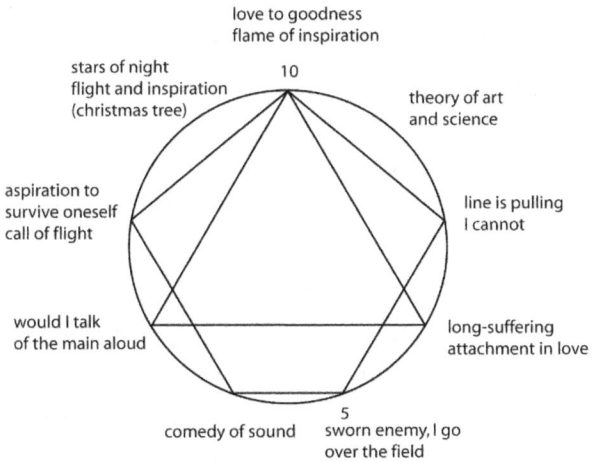

In existence, we meet particular influences having the world around. This way, let us see the factors as they become during tension and limited active powers, because we talk of the subject when it happens. The idea of us being permeated or carriers of having been in love, or applying the subject toward symbolism, becomes here just a love to goodness, but also an inspiration fire. This is a lower level, then initial phenomenon, still carrying for us the meaning of participation and belonging toward higher means. Our human perspective makes us develop ourselves so that we are smart in skill; this gives us Theory of Art and Science, as any level to approach with, having no confidence, so we develop and invent certain rules not to be in a pit. Third step is the entry, or the place of other influences coming. Here it is applied to our world. Around us there is a lot, and we are already overloaded. This way when we are attracted, we feel incapability to submit, and still we are submitting. There is also another side to it; it might be easier to submit for what does not demand from us too much. So, we don't talk of the feeling, which would change it, or deep involvement; here it is clearly the working interval. Either our powers enter, or we are going down. We, theoretically, should experience only sweetness in love, but during daily life, with the efforts of job activity and general work, this becomes a habit, even if we do not want it. We continue and this leads to sliding down, no manifestation of the high, as it needs bigger application of feeling and efforts; however, it is about *conscious* appliance, as we spend even bigger efforts on this stretch of relationships. Then, instead of cares, it is hate and all kinds of complaints and feelings of misfortune. As it's still the same, it is just wording, all is pacified, put under the veil of social stability, like that. This, as it is a subconscious act, leads to our not manifesting anything that might apply us toward exchange, so it is, instead of renewal, self-preservation and aggravation of our state—now we cannot talk of it. Out of this state appears the state of separation; therefore a call of flight and aspiration to survive oneself on a physical level. Out of the dark sky, there are starry lights shining even if you don't remember, and there are points of inspiration and passion to fly—the fabric of inactivity.

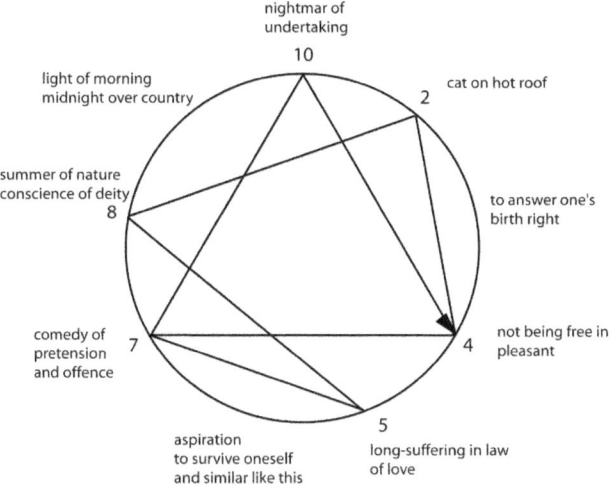

This is a phenomenon of the whole process, with functional application. As it is clearly functional, the period of movement of inner consideration, plan is from ten, with correspondence to *do*, the beginning of octave. This way, it is *Nightmare* of undertaking, instead of abstract content of love, and attraction to higher things in existence. Here we discuss in theory our sexual activity. It is participation on the usual level. Without higher aspirations, search of ideal, etc. We involuntary suffer from cause and result. The tenth stage is the first in terms of it giving us indication on what the scheme is about. This time, one *undertakes* and insinuates a connection. The title presupposes it is out of real factor or it has quite different qualities than we might expect, considering the first two schemes. Out of here, there is an arrow toward the fourth stage, *not being free in pleasant*. This state could be presupposed even by the slogan at the tenth, but its reality might be easily extracted out of the preceding diagram with its long-suffering attachment in love. If we are attached to what we already hardly bear, there appears to be slavery in interaction. Therefore, we come to the second stage, cat on the roof, or the inability to bring everything out of oneself, desire without fulfillment, with inward conflict. This leads to the conservation of certain energetic qualities — the step fixed at eight, we realize. But as long as there is a situation of humanity, society, governmental law, nothing pretty much could be done. We might understand and compose our wishes. But, we need to conform to what is supposed to be permissible. We are obedient to the legality. If it stands before our wish, we suffer. Stage seven, which at the previous scheme was for refusal of talking about, here is a dramatic output. Triangle of 10-4-7 is a triad of accomplishment. It has plan and realization of the very act, reaction, and personification. Transition from five to seven, over the period, means involuntary closing oneself to highest. Then, it is back to the tenth stage in a circle. If we look back toward enneagram, from ten to nine, these are in short terms: what we do (10), our state (2), our position (3), our experience (4), conscious state (5), life's requirements (6), action of personality (7), concentration of powers (8), and common emotional state (9).

PART THREE

Section One

Existential Enneagrams

Enneagram of Door

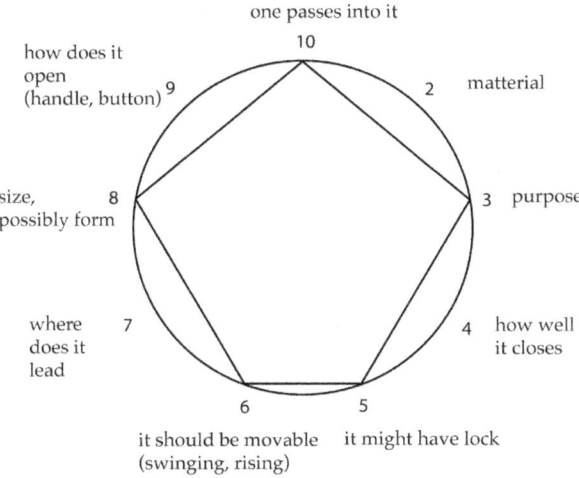

One passes into it
It should lead somewhere, otherwise it is separated from belonging
Somehow it has to open (swing, rise). It might be automatic
It has to fit human height or it is not comfortable (and width)
It might be wooden, plastic, or metallic
It shan't be too thick (has to correspond to purpose [surrounding])
Strong enough; penetration of sound, warmth, air
It has to have a handle to open, or button if it is mechanical
It might have a lock

6 is a crucial point. If the door won't move, we won't be able to use it for its purpose
7 is a meaningful point. We need to go there. This is why we enter.

This is an example of an object taken to enneagramatic scheme. This way we prove that an object of any kind in its totality has or should have nine different factors that would describe its supposed existential meaning. Everyone knows what the door is. If to name all possible considerations, trial is possible to put them into scheme. This is description of an object. Therefore scheme changes in connection it is now used for this. At tenth stage would be placed what actually describes what the object is. Second is for its material, third is purpose, and fourth is for qualities. Five is for possibilities. The seventh stage is for esthetic or meaningful factor. Eight, correction, is for comfort; nine is usage.

Enneagram of Bath

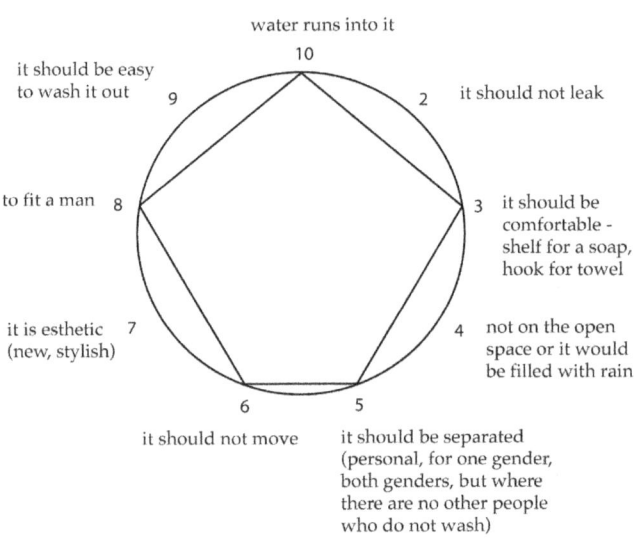

In this scheme, at two, for material, it is standing that *it should not leak*, because this includes the idea of materials from which it is made. Contrary from door, bath should not move. At eight it is the same thing — it should fit a man as a door has to be a particular height for a man to pass. All other stages are different. We can tell that the third stage is more for the subject itself, and the fourth is for its capacity in terms of outside factuality. So, three is about correspondence to what it is for, and four for possibility to stand up for possible influences. In this case, it just *should* be in the interior, or it has something so that rain won't be a problem because otherwise it has such form that it might be filled with rain, and it is not for this. The door should lead somewhere (7); here it is that we come into the bathroom and it is our intentional line. So, it is a bit different. This way, we tell that it might be stylish, in tile, etc., because it should correspond to how bathroom should be like. As the door has to correspond to its placement (for example, in the cavern it might be a foot thick, but in the common room it is an inch or so), so in a bathroom there should be what it is for — to keep soap somehow, where to hang a towel. Its quality is that it is separated, and there is always this feeling of entering the bathroom that it is initial. Nine and six for the door is that it needs to open somehow, and what it is opened with. For bath, as it is not movable and there is no comfort, we talk of things been open or closed, so this includes the idea of getting dirty. For example, the door opens, swings, then closes — there is the idea of movement. Here it is the object used for a shower and bath, so it's on one place, but then you have to clean it. And the door and bath are made for our usage; one presses the button or turns the handle, and we also have to clean the bathtub or it won't be usable anymore.

Enneagram of Boat

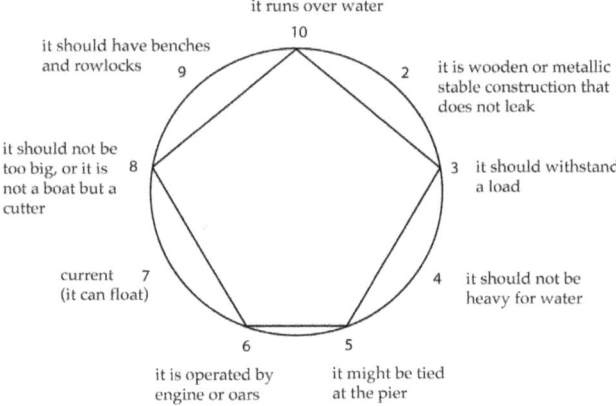

A period from 9 at triangle's corner (1-4-2-8-5-7-10)

It runs over water, for which it shan't be heavy; done from materials so that it won't leak and would be stable, not very big, so that it might be tied at the pier, or it would float away, as it has natural qualities of running over water.

Again, it does not leak. At three it is its quality of being for something, so that it should withstand a load, and at four it is that it should not be heavy for water. This similarity in aptitude should be more developed, but the main thing is, there is always a connection in meaning in between these points, as it is at an interval and the next stage. The fifth situation is that it might be tied; so we know it is a row boat, but the main thing is that each time with different objects, explanations of the objects would be different. But it could be compared with the door, which might have a lock. Here we might consider the initial quality of the door to be locked because for the boat it is either tied or it is on the ground — otherwise it floats. For the door, it might swing open but it is also a question of how well it's locked; this either brings us back to the fourth stage, how well it closes, or this means the door initially presupposes one might not be able to open it. (Where does it lead?) I could have wished to enter, but wasn't able to; it's on the lock. Crucial point at six is that it should be operate-able and that it might float connects it with the idea of direction somewhere, as a door has to lead somewhere or it is not applicable. Currently, the ability to float over it talks about quality, but for the bath it is just that it has an appearance. It should be okay to wash, clean, etc. Eight is for the fact that it is to be operated by man, so it is of relatively small size. That it should have benches and rowlocks is the same thing as for the door to have a handle or button, but it is also connected by meaning with six if it is operated by oars or is opened by a handle (swings).

Enneagram of Bench

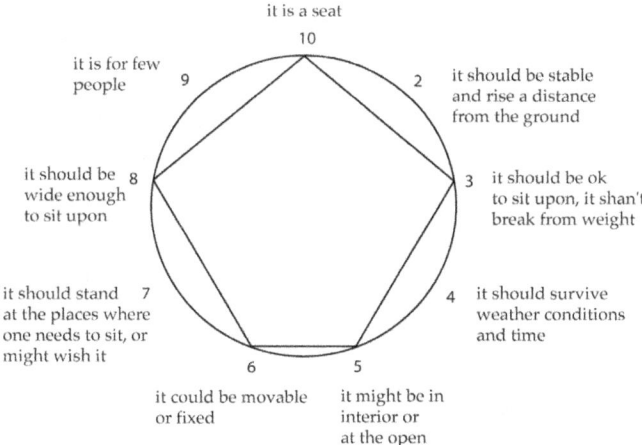

Into the idea of material for the bench, I put that it should be stable and rise a distance from the ground. This is more clear for what bench is, but if it is stable and elevated, this includes how it is built and what it could be used for. From the other side, this doesn't mean yet that it would withstand your weight, so it is put into the next stage; it is different. Also, as it is for a long-term usage, it should survive weather conditions—one cannot make a new bench every season. Whatever the bench is, it might be put inside or outside. This is the character of the fifth stage—that the object doesn't change; it is different kinds not of application but of details. This bench might be movable or fixed, but it talks of it being fallen or removed, so because there is nothing crucial the third station defines it as being stable so that it won't break. So, sixth the crucial point is there might be no bench, as there might be no bath to wash if it is not fixed there. It should stand at the places one might wish to sit at, for waiting, view upon, but this is the point which often might fail — boat can float away, door might not lead prety much anywhere, but it is meaningful point, if it fails, we miss it. It is for seventh stage. Again, for *correction*, there is that it should be wide enough to sit upon. The initial idea of the bench is that it is long enough to sit upon for more than one person. In connection with a crucial point at six, we (two or more) pick it up together, carry, and place it where we want. It would be different for a vertical object, wall for example. It shows us that our representation of three dimensions gets reevaluated considering the application, like verticality to enclose, or using a horizontal plane. Seeing the bench, we would think this is a short bench, or long one. Or, we would tell this wall is really high. Also, if the wall isn't long enough to enclose the area, it makes no sense; or, if the bench isn't above the ground, it is just a plank lying. For the wall, at ten would be a length – how it encloses a certain area, height at nine – its impenetrability, how easy it is to pass it or jump over, and at eight would be its width – for its density to show how strong it is. This way, these three dimensions we are used to think of as equal in practice carry a different informatory load. Such an approach brings the idea of this being possible to look upon from the top of pentagram every step from ten to two in descending sequence to explain the meaning of an object (it is a seat, for few people, wide enough to sit upon, standing at the places where one needs it, movable or fixed, in interior or at the open, to survive weather conditions, good to stand up for weight, from such and such material). It explains the object in details, but initially one starts from naming all possible considerations, and only then putting them to the scheme.

Enneagram of Spirits

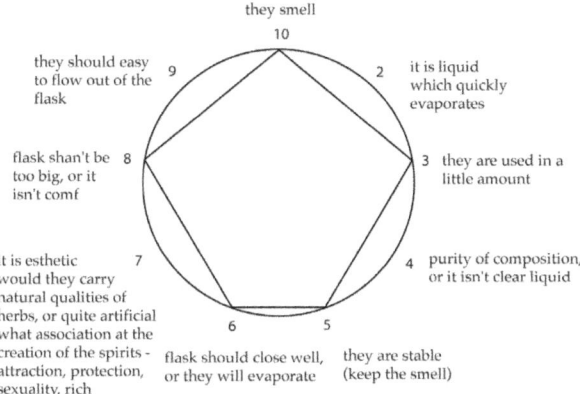

It is liquid, for usage in small amount, in a not-too-big, well-closed flask, which keeps the smell.

This is subject of the spirits. It composes essential qualities of the subject with situational factors. Initially it is what gives a smell. In closer examination, it is quickly evaporating liquid. They are used in a small amount, or there is too much of it. It is quantity. Quality means the composition should be pure, or they won't have transparent consistency. Here we have the idea of quality and quantity—three for *how thick* the door is and four for how well it closes. Five, they are stable, but it also indicates what kind of smell they are in. They might evaporate, so flask should close well, but they also have to flow easily out of it. It shan't be too big, because they are used in a small amount. People use the spirits to associate oneself with the human position. At the creation of the spirits, one might think of them as a means to attract, protect their carrier, to express sexuality, point out their social position — quality of smell, how expensive they are. This seventh stage is for significance. It is esthetic. Their production and composition also means a lot, as well as packaging. They might have an identical smell of herb, or be quite artificial. The fifth stage is not very defined, but as a half to ten, it is its exemplification — they smell, and they have the quality to keep the smell. There is also an exchange of meanings in between five and seven, so for five it is more that there might be different variations of spirits, and seven is our esthetic considerations at usage and creation of spirits.

Enneagram of Nuts

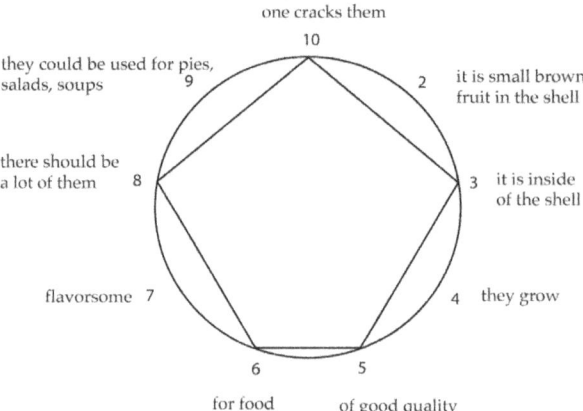

This example is of natural arising. Therefore, there are different considerations, which might fit other similar subjects. Into six, crucial point, enters the realization that it might be spoiled, rotten. Nine is usage; what could be done out of it? Eight here is for multiplicity. We take the nut as belonging to the big pile of nuts, when it is in amount, it is meaningful. (Please look at the functional enneagram of *growing of plants* (p. 11) where there are conditions of the storage of seeds at point two). Four is how good something can stand up to the world outside. For nuts it is if they would grow and how it would occur. There might be different variations of nuts, so we mean some that suit whatever, because people have different tastes. At point three, it is inside the shell, so here is the entry of octave — the shell should be removed, if we want to use it.

In this scheme we can see crucial points, and these points are at the third, sixth, and ninth stage, so that we can begin the story out of them. If we begin from third stage, and go around of circumference it would be as following. Nut is inside the shell (3). It is a small brown fruit inside of it (2). So we crack the shell (10). To use it for food (9). A lot of them (8). We know they are flavorsome (7). To use for food (6); nine was an intention. With such and such taste (5). Coming out of nature (4).

If we begin from the sixth stage it would sound differently. We use it for food (6). They have a quality (5). They grow (4). Inside of the shell (3). A small brown fruite (2). Which we need to crack (10). To use in recepies or just eat (9). And a lot of them (8). As they are flavorsome (7). But, however we try, we cannot continue from other stages, except these; the nature of the stages are clearly defined. Two is for being, what exactly it is. Six is for deterioration and ordering, this way it is for food, then nuts disappear. Seven is for esthetic in existential enneagrams; here there enter ideas of how they receive their qualities from nature, what specifics they carry.

Enneagram of Shades

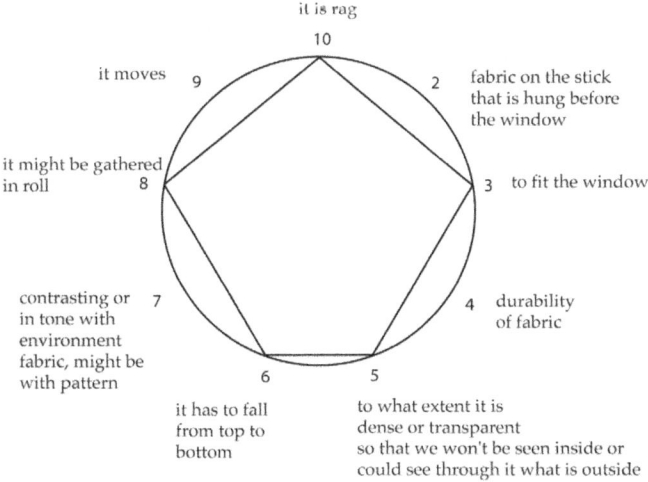

This subject of shades, contrary from previous objects — door, bath, boat, and bench — is of soft quality. We can turn it, roll it, gather it together. It also has the purposeful application to be hung upon the window. This way, initially, drape is actually a piece of rag, so other considerations of its beauty, etc., enter other stages as seven and five. In close considerations, it is fabric, held by the rod, to be fixed above the window (2) to close it, with this possibility (3), or, it might be moved aside (8). As usual, four is for ability to stand up to outside influences, and here it is durability of fabric. It might be dense or transparent in connection with the purpose; it is different from the seventh position, which is undefined, that might be any kind of it, color, etc. Stages seventh and fifth are in interaction. Because stage fifth is for variations. For example, would there be a lock on the door, or possibility to fix the boat. For shades it is if it prevents to see right through. It is done for us, do we want to lock the door for no one to prevent us; do we want or not to be seen from outside. Seven is esthetic effect, how it corresponds to surround, it's not a purpose any longer. So, if we want, it might be removed (8). It is comfortable that we can store it if it is not in need; the difference from nine is that one is an action. The quality of shades is it has to fit the window. It also should continue to do it. It might fit it, but its length also should run all the way from top to bottom. Still, that it would continue, is not warranted, and shades might fall.

Enneagram of Pocket

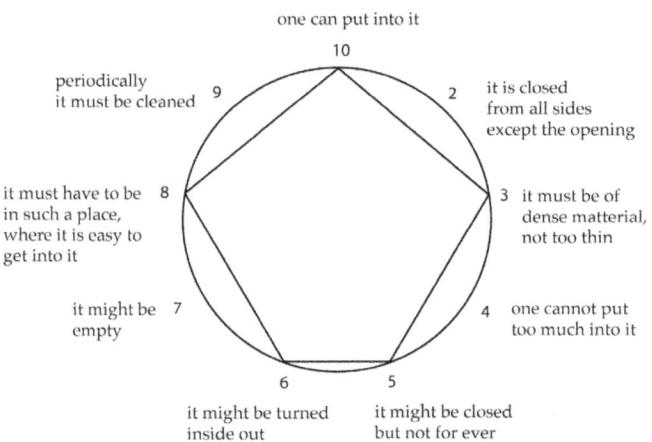

When we think of a pocket, we connect it with something it is attached to. On its own, it is non-existent. As we think of it, it is necessary for putting into it for temporary storage. We know how we find in the pocket old papers and lost articles. Sooner or later, we would discover them, unless the pocket is gone together with what it is a part of. The way a pocket is constructed addresses our requirement to have good pockets, which won't be torn away or detach on its own. Its size is according to where it belongs-. However, it is a delusion to think of it as a means of storage; it is of temporary featuring point for man on the move and impossible to hold in hands everything we might encounter for ever. One of qualities of such conglomeration is — we know it is turn-able. We can pull it and stretch out when it becomes dysfunctional.

Enneagram of Button

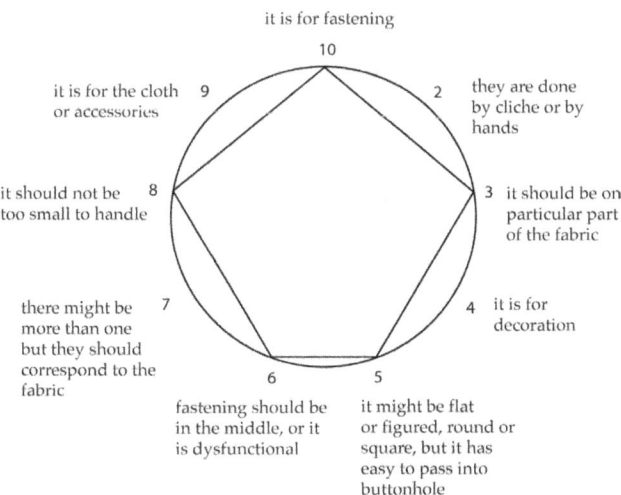

When we think of button, it is already a finished object, article, in its own right in terms of system. It is complete, round, and necessary has holes. (Or fastening). But, in terms of its life around the world, there is or are applications, as it was coming for a destination; however, it might be on its own. It is not necessarily attached to the cloth, etc.

We know how we pick them up, and on the question 'What is it?' tell — oh, it's the button! In this position, they are done by hands or mass production, complete like they are on their own.

Enneagram of Color

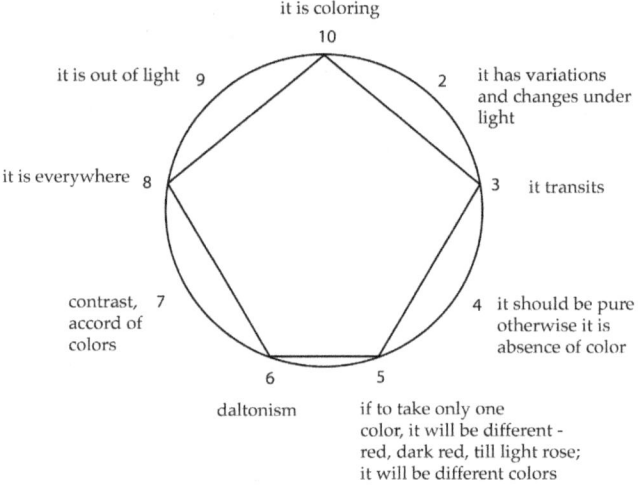

Color is an abstract mentation of man, put into form with different shades on a piece of paper, existing on its own in nature, corresponding to our mentation and appearance of facts. We never see red sky, unless it is dawn. We manage to suppose that color is good or bad in its appearance as *we* perceive it. What is of invariable qualities of color has nothing to do with our perception but with a particular set of special qualities or features. We might not find the words to describe what color really is, but we know it adds the coloring to objects. We might know what mineral or other would give this coloring, but this relates more to the physical aspect of matter, chemistry. To be such as it is supposed, color on its own is something special. It has to be pure, not necessarily bright. It is also not permanent, independent from its physical factor, of possible fading as we perceive it. It is going to be seen differently under different lights — one in daylight and the other in electrical light. Illuminated in the dark room, it might seem very bright or soft. We might be incapable of being sensitive enough to see some of the color wave stages, or to discriminate them. Colors might be done in accord when put together, or they would awake a feeling of pressure; attitude is not the same for everyone. If to know what kind of color we wish to picture, we can stretch it from light to dark, so that it would lose its possibilities to be called by one name, but still it is from one color. Color has physical aspects. It is impossible to reproduce all kinds of color with paints. It is done with the help of highlights and darkening. If there is too much of grey in the color, it looses its purity. A big skill is required in putting in colors so that they will reproduce true relationships of objects, and yet would have an esthetic look. Few colors might be mixed together in gradations so that it would transit from one shade to another. The preliminary condition for color is we need a light for it, as it has to do with white ray.

Section Two

Enneagram of Sex and Aging

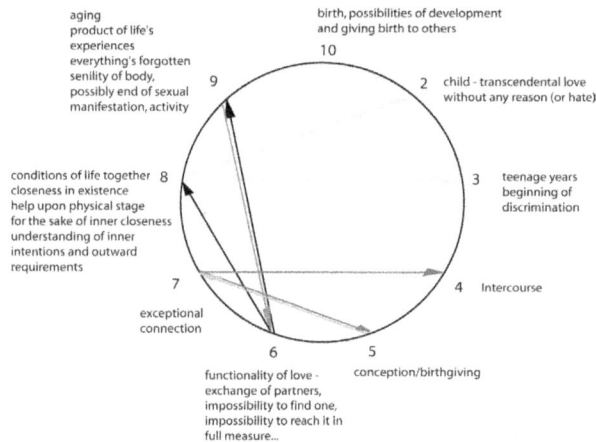

The process of age is an option. If we get old, we cannot avoid aging; we follow. The indication over the scheme can help us view the process in its connections because the value of one stage is transmitted for another. This process of exchange of qualities in this way as it is indicated on this scheme, is only for phenomena that we cannot exchange. This way, it goes from bigger numbers (from nine to five) to smallest, because there is a difference in between of two sides of enneagram, one from the right of us is for existence. This way, it comes from some that initiate control toward existentiality. However, it is only assumption. Scheme doesn't talk of it. Everything is taken upon one level, because it's taken as existential phenomena. However, we cannot do anything about necessary to get aged. The difference from sequential enneagram is even though there is a sequence in time from childhood to old age, there are some processes which are in time and then interactions after some level is reached. When we get old, these interactions do stop and lose their importance. When we become an adult, we finally reach the possibility to accept intercourse in its character. It is the fourth stage upon the scheme. After this, development is done and other stages carry different configurations. After the intercourse, it is the possibility of conception or pregnancy, depending upon gender. The next three stages are of accidental and improvement. When an arrow points, it means that there is the quality of that stage from which an arrow goes and it is interesting to see the correspondence in between those stages that have arrows from the same source.

Enneagram of Doors

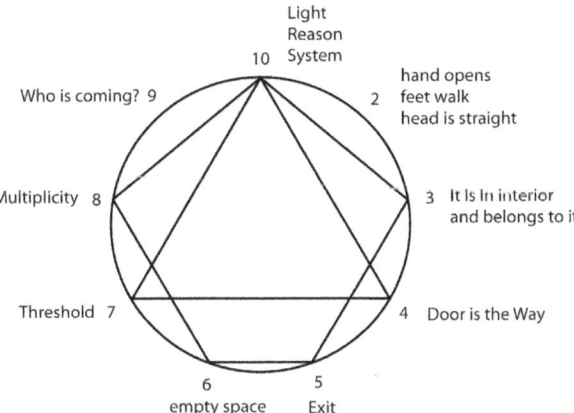

The subject of a door could be taken from a different perspective with the idea of it being abstract. This is symbolism. Now it is not about a door — a wooden or plastic object used for passing out of one room into another; it is a symbolic idea of a passage, not of any passage, but where it leads to, etc. To discuss the stages, we need to come away from initial enn. Door is a way. It is also an exit if one wishes to run away, or it might be closed (it might have a lock, so it's five). There should be empty space or it won't move. It is a threshold (where does it lead). When we open the door, we have a particular attitude. Our hand turns the handle, we step across, and we look ahead at the possible hindrance or another man coming. Multiplicity — there are a lot of doors. Here it is philosophical subject that we can view as a symbol. We can also apply it also to any idea of passing and finding. This process is different and yet it corresponds to this plan. It would be then a modal enneagram, which is getting explained farther on. The difference from three kinds of enneagram is, if existential is just for the door, as an object, which closes the entrance, for symbolic we can say Door is a Way. For modal, it would be an idea of any passage, not even a door. If we would take a door without its application completely, for example place it amid the room, without it leading anywhere, as for installation art, it would give us the view upon it, as experiential enneagram, also discussed later. That is, we would just experience the door in its material.

Farther on there are examples of symbolic enneagram of salt, and modal enneagram of sugar. We think of them as condiments, but they are clearly different, not just opposite of each other. Sugar is rather submissive. It is too sweet. If to take it in too much, one would get sick. The bakery needs it. Salt is required on its own. With sugar it is second hand — it's not that we need it, it is that the bakery would be impossible without it.

Enneagram of Salt

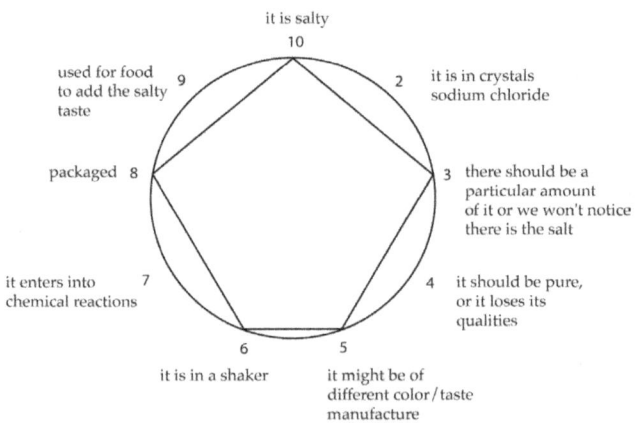

Next two enneagrams — existential and symbolic enns on the theme of salt. If to review an existential enn, all stages are clear in coordination with previous schemes of the same kind. Symbolism is a matter of metaphor. Salt adds a salty taste. Estimation of qualities might approach understanding the requirement of what is *not* out of close necessity (because one might not put salt into food to be filled). However, if it is put into it, it might give addiction. Association in between food taking, done for life, as a necessity, and life, not necessary ideal, is at hand. There is interplay in between literary realization of things and its objective quality. Addiction is an outcome when we use it often because we estimate, but for estimation we need to reevaluate. This way, it is what it is — crystals of sodium chloride, having salty taste, therefore used for food, then – as it is used often, we received it *packaged*. In this package, we have one and the same salt, but we know it is like a dust, so it is *unity in multiplicity*. It is always disappears, and we can register this. It has to be mixed up with other components, and has participation, if we use it. It is a role-playing game. We might never have salt, or it needs to be at hand, so it is in a shaker. We know how we often look for this at the table. It's a requisition. Clarity of salt might, however, have qualities not interceding with it. We don't mean clear sodium chloride; depending upon where it is coming from, salt would have traces of minerals, other acquisition, in dependence upon production. However, at symbolic diagram, it is not a character that it also carries apart from being salty, but just a trace. One leaves it everywhere, here and there. In story tales salt often is said to be used for marking the way. Qualities, then, are at four. When we think of salt, we see the application of a little pinch, but if there is not a significant amount of it, it isn't available; this way, it might be gone.

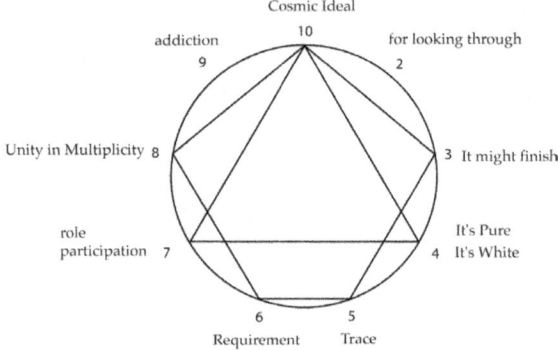

Enneagram of Balcony

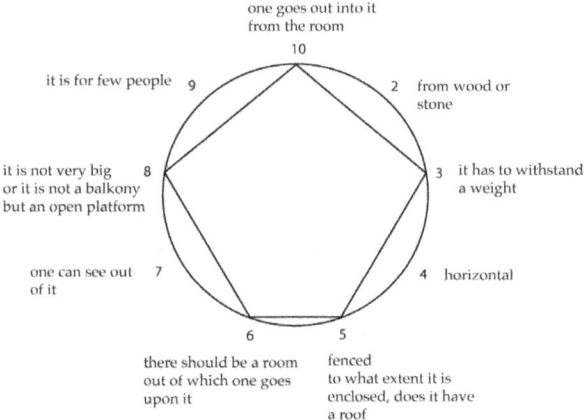

A pentagram

It is possible to get out on it from the room, which we have; it is not so big but should withstand our weight; and it is still enclosed, just partly enclosed in comparison with the room

A period

When we step out of the room into the balcony (10 → 4) this balcony is as if continuation of the room. It isn't something completely different. The fact that it is horizontal includes the idea of how it is done, it's construction, and the beams on which it is placed. (4 → 2) It is made of wood or stone. This point also includes how it is fixed so that it won't fall. At point eight it is said that it is just a small balcony, so that even though these materials from which it is made have significant weight, a relatively small amount of them was used and it is not too heavy to be secure. (2 → 8) Balconies are always fenced. It is done for the fact that there isn't a lot of space; and they are elevated so that this point also should include the idea of elevation (8 → 5).

It might be enclosed, but it is so our view won't be blocked. (5 → 7). It is connected with the room (7 → 10).

exit out of the room into balcony	from 10 to 4
construction	from 4 to 2
how it is fixed	from 2 to 8
balcony is elevated	from 8 to 5
possibility to receive impressions	from 5 to 7
data and memory	from 7 to 10

Phenomenal Enneagram of Room

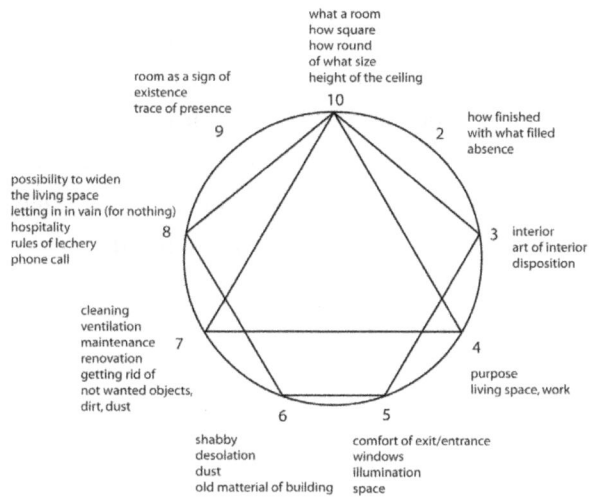

Phenomenal enneagram of room. Next there is existential and higher existential (symbolic). We are going to review all stages from a different perspective to see the correspondence and difference. In a phenomenal enneagram into ten enters everything we can tell of the room, of its very subject. What the room is like, its size, would it be square or round. This is not an application to one room in particular. For the second stage of this kind of enneagram, goes what might be usual for it. Room should be finished, filled with this or that. From another side, it might be unfinished yet, or empty, without a furniture. (Please look ahead at the existential room enneagram, points six and seven—there is the difference). After what is *usual* for the room, there is a particular application; here (for the room) it is the possibility of design, but also what the interior is like. Then it is its designation—whom is it for. In a way, we have to see this stage as what rooms could usually serve. Five, the joy, is comfortableness of it (or it being uncomfortable). Everything that makes a room desirable—the position of the windows, light, perspective; this is stage of accommodation. Sixth are drawbacks of dissolution, dispersal. It is limited (a dissolution) by the fact that it has still continued to remain a room. Seven—cyclic turn over requirement, necessity to clean, ventilate, because it is getting filled with dust, accumulation of garbage, or it might be renovated. Eight is a place, not very necessary, but with its own features corresponding to the entry of octave, without it this would be impossible. A room cannot exist without certain interactions. We exit, enter, come and go, let people in, lose them (absence), call them to invite. At nine, a human factor, it is how it corresponds to the fact that it is (was) occupied.

Existential Functional

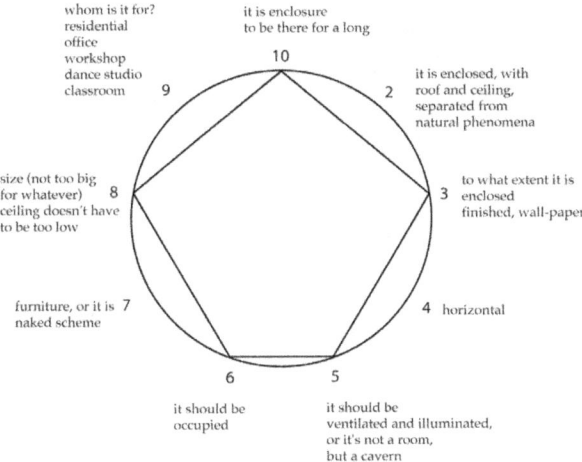

Higher Existential

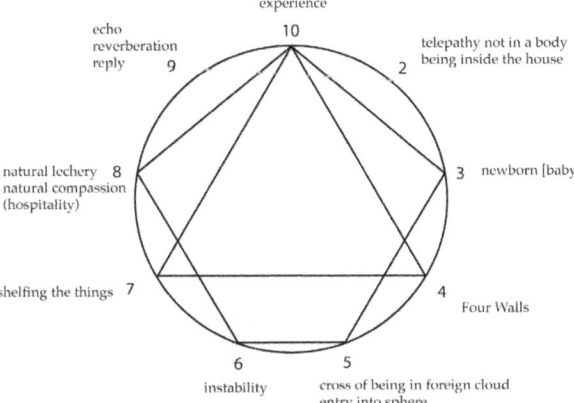

In comparison of two schemes, factual and symbolic, we can see correspondence of meaning in between stages for one and the same figure of both schemes. For example, ten — as long as we are somewhere for a long, it is experience. Of course, different choices of meaning might be chosen for symbolic reasons, which cannot be said about the factual. It speaks about the difficulty of philosophical subjects, our personal attitude toward requirement, things in general terms — all this is predefined, however, by what we may feel about subject, this time, the room. We can see it very differently: possibly a comfortable place, shabby, newly painted, anything. Why should we choose these or that for it? We know we might see things in its nine components. Finding the explanation of actual upon some level of symbolic reasoning does not prevent us from later make a comparison. We can take a step farther and tell the room is a box where vibrations and different wavelengths are reverberated. This way, it is an echo, a reply. We know how we are hit by the influences when we enter the space, so the difference from nine and ten is ten is our personal experience if nine is a totality for the room. This way, as it is influenced, it is 'whom it is for?' — a human factor of nine, not the fact that it is separated space (2).

Enneagram of Plastic

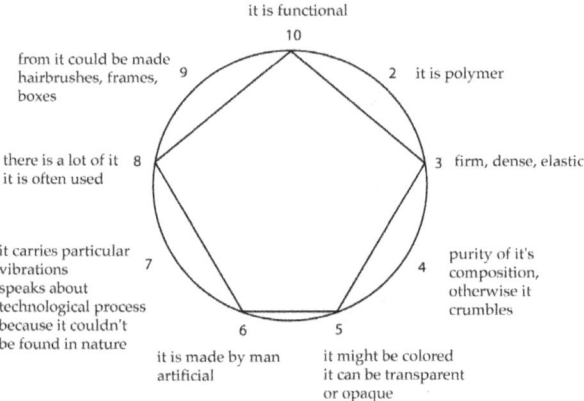

Plastic, in its form, is a supple material, fabricated for usage of mass production. Our technology gives as the possibility and knowledge of how to produce such things, which are from synthesized raw material. We might address the question of technology. What is required from production is to produce it so that it would withstand outward pressure and time, even if it is corrupted faster than for example metal. As it is artificial, it carries certain vibrations of its fabrication — it often smells, also not very precious but sometimes of good quality and required at this place. Exchangeability. Technological process involves solution for ecological and maintenance problems. The line of production, how adequate it is. Also search of how to manage with waste materials, and other. As an often used object, it is produced in multiplicity, in different densities, depending on targeting destinations.

An Angel Cake

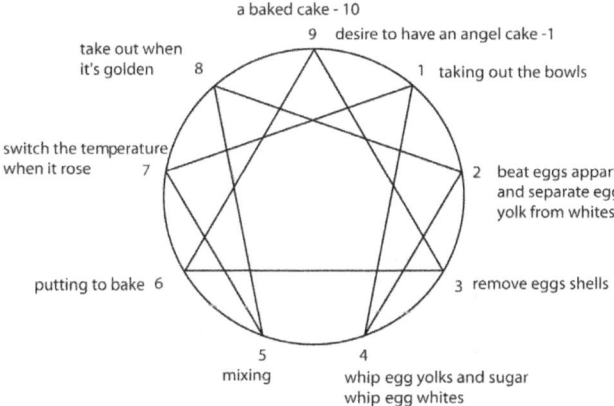

There are two enneagrams about baking an angel cake — one is functional and another just sequential. Let us discuss the period first. When we take out the bowls, we do this knowing we are going to put egg whites in one and yolk in another. The second stage, when it is beginning, is done for the final result. Whipping of yolks and whites happens after we had separated them at the second stage. When we mix, we make it to be of one consistency, then it is good for baking. Point seven, when we are waiting for it to be done, is connected with the initial stage of one, because during this time one can wash these bowls, which we took before. So, this is the end of the first octave, which could be called mechanical. At the triangle, it is throwing away an eggshell, which is always done. At the same time, it is the beginning of making a cake. Then we put to bake. The start of the process is initiation out of our wish and the result is a baked cake upon a plate.

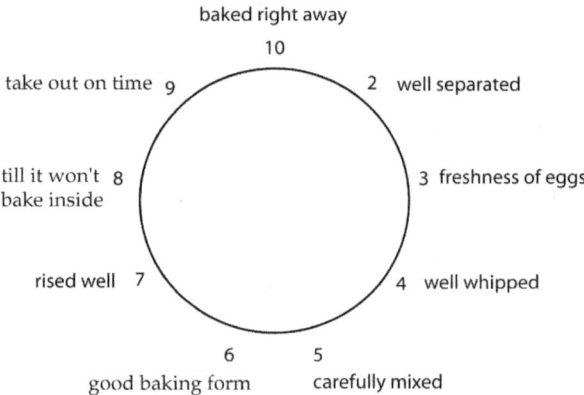

The sequential diagram consists of crucial points of process. It should be baked right away, or maybe on time, to have it. Yolks should be well separated from whites. Eggs should be fresh. We could see the correspondence of the same numbered stages of these two enneagramatic schemes on the same subject.

Enneagram of Mountains

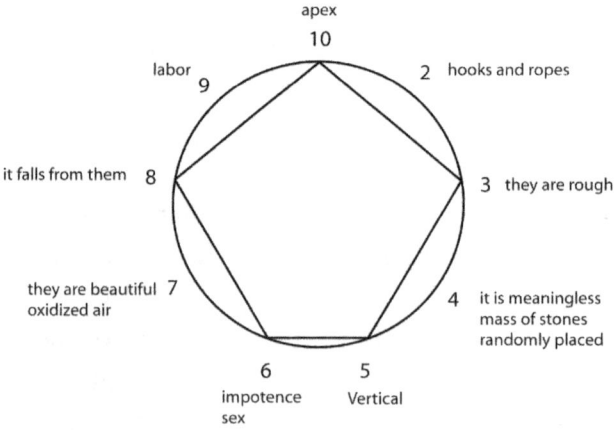

Mountains are an indispensable part of our nature, something we think of too often. Sea and wind are primary securing powers of our world; in participating with them, we touch the element of emptiness and fulfillment and they are complete. When we consider our human situation, one always goes to these securing points of natural elementary giants. We know we are alone. Without all establishments, the world is gone. We are obliged to continue; it is a question of effort. Anyway, we know we can consider a mountain from the point of view of continuation because as stabilization, it does not make sense. We might not even consider it. As it is meaningless, for what we do should require need or meaning of action, we might believe this to be up to the point that one should think of it in these terms, of it belonging to continuation, of change. In this way, as part of human interactions, they also get addressed as the symbolic meaning of our abstract mentality — an explanation. One can do this differently. Here, it is a trial to gather under one roof; what is possible is of a different appearance but answers the position of the mountain in our scheme of what things should be or are.

This way, it is an apex. The highest point of the big mass of stones, esthetical and healthy to intercede with. If we go up on them, it requires as labor so and tools with which it is done. Three and eight are places of struggle and situation. The situation does not necessarily require a struggle so they are connected in this way. As a pentagram for existence, an apex involves verticality (10 and 5). Five here is the predisposition or halfway toward the beginning or source. Verticality and elevation answers the question of gravitational nature—it is sliding down rocks; they fall as other objects do. There is a particular feeling toward rocks and cliffs; they are rough and we produce a certain effect (6). It is symbolism.

Enneagram of a Book

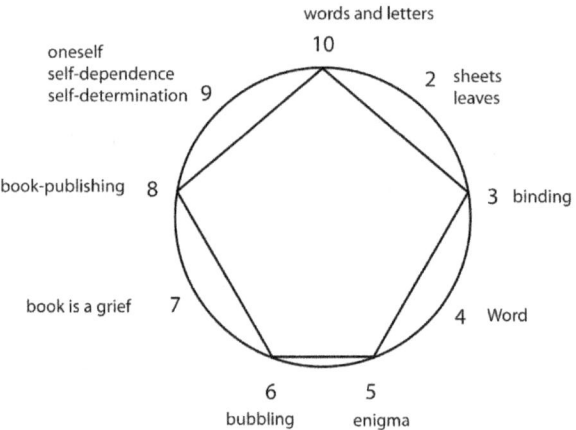

For the book, it is a comparison of general meeting terms; its physical aspect (10, 2, and 3), aspect of content, contextual (4, 5, 6), and action (7, 8, 9). It is words and letters, upon the leaves, in a bound; it is open in terms of its enclosure of meaning, its factuality is unclear, and this is output; a lot of work is required to make it through, there is a company who leads production, market, it is on its own yet we choose it. It is published and we brush the leaves, yet it is an enigma yet (8, 2, 5). It is someone's empowered action, in binding on the shelf; we might wish to pull it up (6, 3, 9). A lot of words are required to pass through us to get the meaning, and it is a hard job.

Enneagram of a Woman's Character and Will

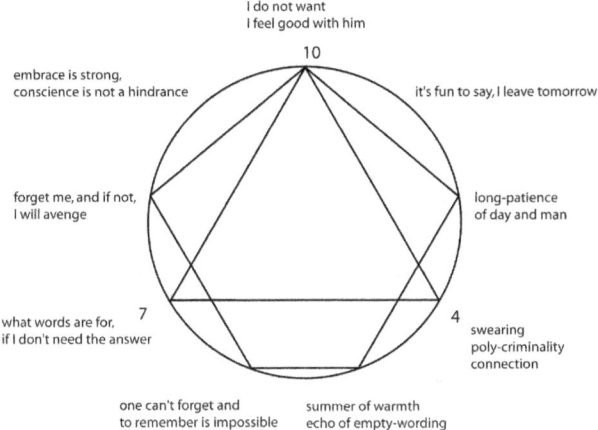

This enneagram belongs to the deep roots of a woman's personality. We know some of the things that might be applied, but what was used should be connected together to form the scheme. There should be direction in this common intention, ready to supply a woman's character.

For the ten, it has two sides of intention as it is manifested and it is manifested emotionally to be strong enough. It has positive and negative factors. Steps around it go according to this with repulsion on the right and activity on the left in pairs. Slogan at nine means she doesn't care of anything else as long as she is attracted. It's opposition at two is she's going away as she has nothing in common. If to look from this second stage in connection with a periodic line, 2 → 8, as she's going, she wants to be forgotten. Her reaction is forceful; she cannot wait. For the opposing factor, contrary to it, it is long-long patience, just of life; my whole life is patience (of day and man).

Slogan at seven, at left corner of the base of the central triangle, might relate to common attitude, not necessary of hetero. She isn't confused about her choice. We often do not want to listen when it is clear for us what we chose. We don't need anything else, no other explanation of why we should turn somewhere our attention.

We already have what we want and do not want what we dislike. This is the meaning of line seven through ten. Seven is intentional, someone's belonging. Four, its opposite factor, is slavery. It is a swamp where she'd stuck. There is a connection to explain and justify. For it is used the word criminality. It is placed there in connection with that fourth is for legality. Swearing means she's pretty much in it.

At the sixth stage, which used to be called transition, it is that it is neither here nor there, but it's a continuation, so this slogan is used therefore. There are a lot of things happening, and we might consider such a possibility. Fifth stage I called the novelty at the beginning of the book. Three is a place where something could be added. In this scheme there is nothing to enter. So, three is the routine. At four there is no change, she's stuck there. This way at five, it is what used to be, the same thing, only peaceful. But there is some intentional deception.

Theorem of Beauty and Dust

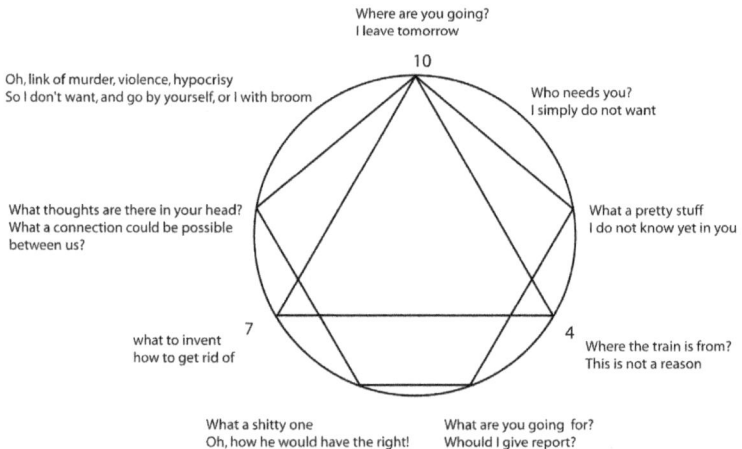

Here is the talk put into the enneagramatic scheme in between two people — one feminine and the other masculine gender — with inclination into a bigger conflict. This way, the second line is a girl's reply to the man's question, and we hit the talk when there is already opposing directions. The woman wants to keep her own way and be free, and there is a pressure upon this from the man's side. We might see particular stages or interplay of forces behind each question and answer, but this is not so important as the flow of process itself. There is really a development, and we may wish to imagine a particular prehistory, also some final, but these are not the part of *this* process. As the predisposed part, it is that she's already going (initial stage at ten). Second is for situations and conditions. Whatever are the conditions, she's posed before the question to face her inability and be humiliated. From another side, if *he* really believes her unworthy, there won't be a reason to insist and turn attention. She needs it not. She might be happy without it, and she just wants to go on her way. This puts emphasis on certain indicative points because this means she's worthy. The meaning of her answer is that she doesn't want it not because someone else needs her. So, it's not about *her* being picked up, it is that she chooses her preference. Process continues, because there is some mistake. He says he doesn't need her. She says she just doesn't want. In a way, her response is correct. But it means she's nervous because of the pressure. Third stage is not a flirt, it's a rude thing to say after her refusal. Her response to this means she doesn't understand yet what role he plays just being around. The question at four is something of self-defense and the same type of attack. It is digging out. Her answer means she leaves not because of some business but just leaves. *What* are you going for? She doesn't believe *he* has the right to ask. Then he is cursing and she tells him he has no right to do that. Seven is for production, so to continue it is what it is. At eight he questions her essence, and she ask what could she have in common with him. He explains and she tells him she doesn't want it and will defend herself.

Section Three

Enneagram of Sex and Belonging; Mutual Connection

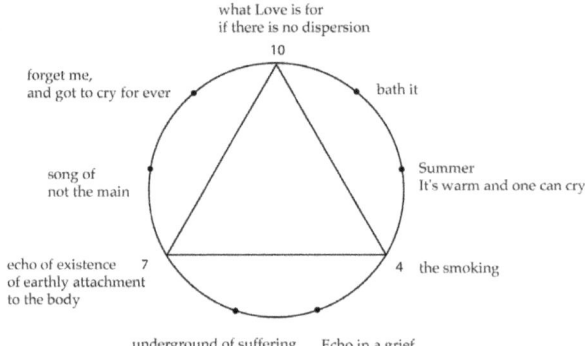

We know that love might be reciprocal. It is supposition. Let's take an example. When both people experience one and the same feelings toward wholeness of event, all the feelings coincide and there is also participation in the same actions. Seven is appreciation of each other's body structure. Ten, five, and six is conscious, emotional, and subconscious, inward reactions or attitude to things. Nine is the result, appreciated before parting. Two and three are for sensual aptitude. Four and eight are inclusion for both man and woman into the art of the interactive game. Over the circumference run steps — how they come in time. At first there is the meeting of people with the same odd, mental intuitive direction, then they coincide into each other's company and they feel the sensation of being together. Then they interact to make a stay together longer (4). They feel vibration of similar tonality (5). Then it comes deeper than just existential passivity (6). Then they might have a sex, or it's just a sexual feelings, scheme doesn't talk of this (7). So, outwardly they continue or prolong the situation, so that it won't slip away (8). At ninth stage there is a parting. Periodic line gives idea of interactions. From ten, inward intellectual considerations and emotional inclinations, it goes to participation together (two). This coming together isn't much required by life. Meaning of this line is desire to suppress disbelieve into possibility of love. Out of this action, there is a link with being together; the line indicates the appearance of pull and they come into each other's sphere. From two to eight is the realization of the reaction inside so that it should be hidden. There is the memory of real factors of true attachment or compassion to another, the partner, from eight to five. From five to seven it is the desire of realization if it is so significant, the thing. Then it is the pull back of acquisition of habit of character to be inclined to the state at ten. This way, action continues and all was mutually experienced and appreciated.

Enneagram of Periodical Meeting

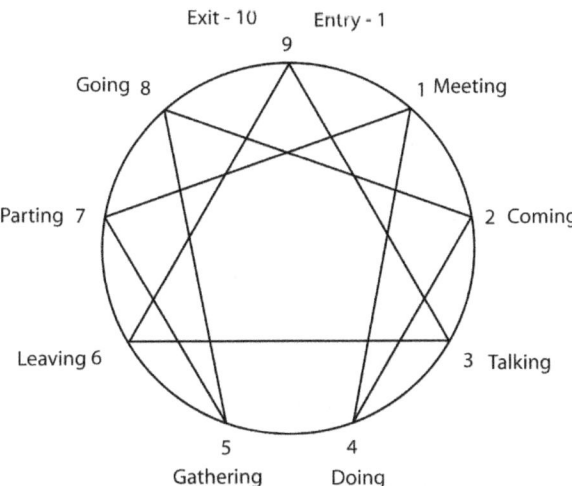

Enneagram of periodical meeting is when people come for the event. It is required entry toward one, or participating, then one is met at the meeting place. They come at the place of the event. They talk together. It is done what was planned. Then they gather to leave. They leave, part ways, and return (going). Exit—event is done.

Modal Enneagrams

In modal enneagram there is no pentagram. There are three triangles and the periodical inner line of connection works. Period: Cause-decision-slowing-overcome-realization-final. Triangle out of the period: Whole-factor-reverberation. Transcendence-slowing-knowledge. Source-fruition-decision.

In this model we see factors as they work in general for modal enneagrams. There is a model, which is used for any thing or activity. Our wish is to find out how it could be used in understanding. The difference in what could be called symbolic (what is called higher existential before) and modal tempo is dramatic. If symbolic is something, which was torn from its direct application and could be used to similar formation, even abstract mentation in general, modal enneagrams from one side are always an application but much farther from the subject than it is even with symbols. It gives the possibility of usage of enneagramatic explanations for subjects, not laying into any other interpretations. At the same time, it would also have elevated and symbolic pictures for stages on the diagram; they would speak of things in general. This is what is its model. If symbolic enneagram has its roots from the visible world, modal enneagrams descend from abstraction into the visible to make for the work of forces. The process, as it starts, begins from above, and if it is a subject, not event, then it has the source from nature of the subject. Over the circumference, we have source-totality-transcendence-resultant-reflection-informatory nature-will power-factors of situation and slowing. If it is ascending, then out of slowing, coming into the situation, there is an entry of octave of our wish, leading to the decision, and after the gathering of information, by the means of reflection of initial forces, we come to suffering, then we transcend it and receive the prize, then we are out on the market.

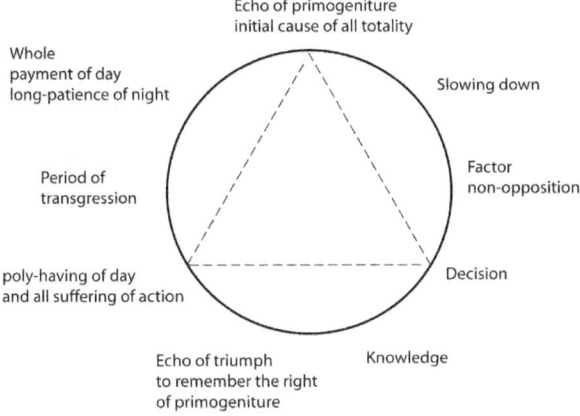

Enneagram of Echo (Vibrations)

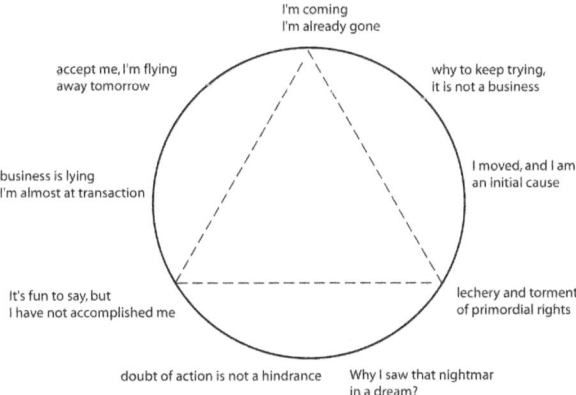

Let's see an example of modal enneagram of the vibratory factor. We take any vibrations of sound or coming forces. Ten is a compilation of nature of appearance. In this case it is a transitory nature. Nine or totality for vibration is that it is very impermanent and also that we have to perceive it. The movement of vibration or its pressure consists of the fact that it is always almost done and also is very passive. The result is never out of order because it does not bring results, unless it is destruction, as with an earthquake or explosion, but there are other forces in action. Being reflective in its nature, vibrations work apart from being useful or meaningful or not. They have a possibility to be insolent or incomprehensive, without clear deciphering at hand. Their nature is also the master and executioner; they manifest under the laws that bring them into existence and transports emanations. Their circumstances are that at the same time vibrations are the cause and what is moving. Their weak point is, it doesn't really make sense, as in music, it might be esthetic, then it is for excess.

Enneagram of Mountains

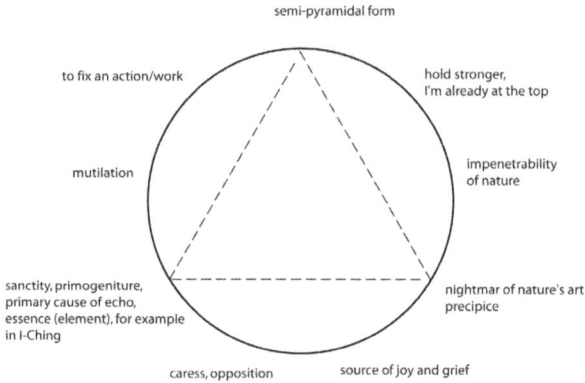

Here it is possible to apply to any apex; it is disconnected from the applied fact.

Before there was enneagram of mountains that was symbolic. This one is modal and it has another taste to it. Please note that scheme or its character remains very similar in between of existential, symbolic, and modal enneagrams, or rather we can find the parallels in between of what is at a third for example stage of existential enneagram and at the third stage of symbolic one. When we try to compose enneagram, it is easier to begin from putting it as an object (existential), and they find symbolic parallels, but trying not to mistaken it with what could be a modal.

If to take the existence of mountains, it will be:

10	Natural formation, element of earth
2	They consist of basalt, etc.
3	They might be weathered, but still they are firm and solid
4	There might grow something
5	There might be exploitation of ore
6	There could be earthquake, volcanic feature
7	They protrude upon the earth's surface
8	They are of big size, not just hills or cliffs
9	One can go around them, or make a rout

It is taken for better cognition of the subject. Please look at the scheme where it is symbolic to make a comparison. Two is situation, what holds us back. Three is quality. Modal enneagram is of another kind of approach. It is consisted from components taken in its nature together. Of course there are inner octaves. If we look closer at the inner octaves, we can make up the difference in between the two systems. For example, for symbolic enn, second stage would consist of tools, act, and doer. In the modal the slogan at second means an intentional fixation. It is taken out of the frame of mountain as a subject. It is reworked for a trial to hold on stronger toward something you try to reach, and coming. In both schemes, factors carry voice of having just considered to do so, and applying efforts, and on another side one's emotions at doing. Its opposite factor, at station nine, is where initially labor comes from physical requirements and is done without a personal approach. Quality here is its solidity, and possible harm from it (third and eight). Two opposing factors at the lower stages of enn, fifth and sixth, speak a lot about participation of natural forces. At these stages they coincide and oppose each other. Obviously, any apex, if to take symbolically, would give the idea of being high (verticality), and at six, *impotence and sex*, it gives the idea of resourcefulness and passing of any ability to. If we overcome something, it is out of our effort by means of capability, but the initial starting point comes from somewhere; it is not initiated by efforts or talent. At symbolic scheme stage seven is human reaction. It is qualities of esthetic and resourcefulness. For example, air components. In the modal it is apart from us being applied to it. We use the terms to explain it. Its subject could be stretched very high, as abstract idea. It stretches to the primary nature of physicality. It is easy to make up a symbolic scheme out of the existential, but they should not be confused with modals. In modal enneagrams, explanations of the stages are more about pictures; it could be drawn by placing little pictures at its stage. For example, with mountains, pyramid at 10, or bicycle for 8 (one falls from it and might harm oneself). Sun at five, as the source of joy and pain; butterfly — both caress and opposition; stairs for seven — an initial order of things where there is ascending. The long carpet for the second station, as a flat surface which we traverse. This way, if a symbolic subject is taken and approaches its higher meaning, here it is that higher meaning approaches the subject; there is function of our mind, permitting us to see things and objects in terms of particular meaning, not symbolic, but explanatory. It is very often that one feels it in childhood; all this might enter later into associations with those meaning which might be applied. Therefore, it is very difficult to be impartial in these terms, because we already have associations with the meaning of objects. This as anything else gives the possibility to exhibit not a quantity but quality. Looking at the plate, for example, we notice how it's different from others. Its size, pictures on it. From modal point of view, plate is a flat, round, solid, impenetrable for liquid. This pictures it from quite another view. It is often used upon the manufacturing plants, and mentation of technician has a particular keen for this. Or, for example, a picture of a year in a round form, as a cycle of changing seasons, it is a wheel. A western man is incapable of truly appreciating, with his mentality, such things. It is the outlook, which we used to have or which is in use of certain cultures, less educated, without ledges of accumulated informatory knowledge.

Enneagram of Sound of Flow of Love

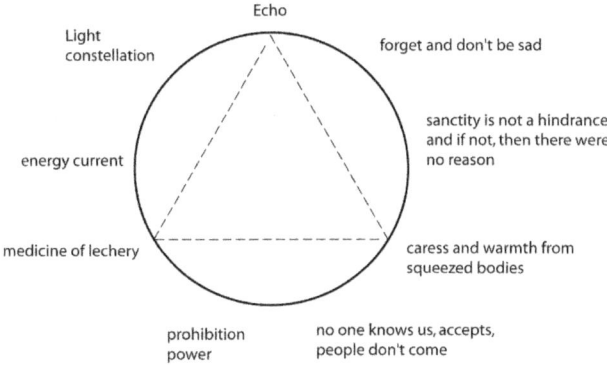

Let us take the example of semi-abstract faction to view it differently from a subject or artificial objects. It is the objective phenomenon of us hearing what we do not see, and it is an exemplification of the total process of making love. Love is going on, and we can hear. Here is a model of this totality of phenomenon. Vibrations go first as the initial factorial statement. At nine it is the totality (constellation) of factors, which relate to the act of empowerment. For transition, it is the current of energy that passes throughout our body during this time. This is an indication of the importance of this factor for the process because energy always circulates in us. At the place of the factor of realization, there is *medicine of lechery* (what is of factual sensors of us); it explains this stage as being not so much an abstract factuality in it qualification, but as something direct that immediately has to do with the present transaction. Our reaction, and of the world around us, is that there is always a feeling of inadequacy; we are always guilty and are trying to remove this emotion at least at the moment of intercourse. We can feel that it never will be permitted; from another side there are powers involved in such things, which move us on. It is akin to the human right by birth to have such things. At the place of knowledge, which was also called realization, there are a few sentences. It is fifth stage, its meaning is, two people are alone, with no one else around. They are in solitude, but there is a feeling of possible coming of other people, because people might have come. But at this moment there is no other communication. The decision here is for doing, it is not an agreement, it is a decision to participate in this kind of action. The factor (the third stage) is that if it is done, it has not been hindered by religious considerations, and if it is not done, then there are no reasons for doing, not because of the above mentioned considerations, like associations with grief or vice of commitment, as it is sometimes put in words in religious literature. Second stage is for slowing. We can view it as parting and going away. But at this moment we temporary forget of this fact. In this way, what is aright on enneagram is for action taking place, and what is on opposite, at left, is for processes about how they feel inside us. If to take a period it is common acceptance of each other (10), then it is the act (4) and we enjoy it (2); there is an energetic reaction in one (8) we feel now after a bit of a process when we are partly back to ourselves' totality of the whole situation and our placement in it (5), then it is sex, as it is described or experienced (7), and out of it we come back to the fact of common totality, maybe unification.

Enneagram of the Flow of Business in Time

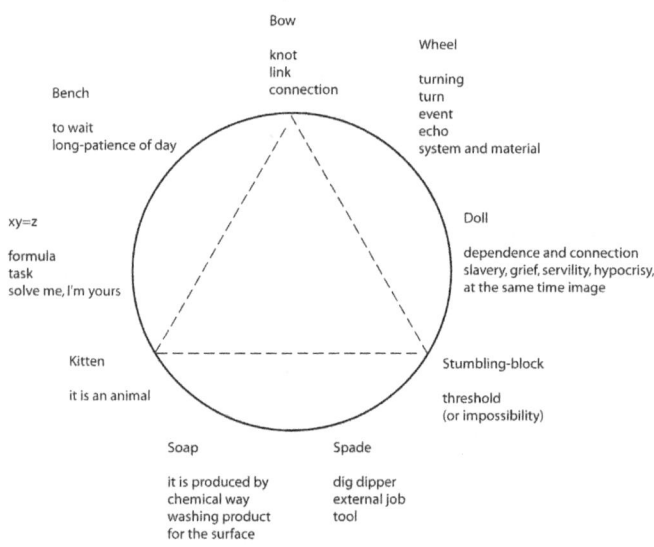

Story of Enneagram

In this diagram are used terms and pictures. The idea of it is in general terms of business processes. Nine, the bench, answers the fact that there is always a momentum in business when there is no move; it is a time of expectation of the result or right period for the next transaction. Doll is for personality with all that follows from this term — pretension and obliging powers of dealings inside the society. At the sixth station, word soap is used to indicate that in any business we have to deal with consequences of any job where something is processed. For example, at the process of manufacture, there always is a waste material that needs to be removed or dissolute. Periodic sequence. Any process is put into work for something, even if it is recurrence (wheel — 2). This includes consequences of starting a process, it should go on. Then, the system is shaken by the fact there is a start. And, there is a change in material. Something is brought in to work upon. Initially, as with computers, there is some stabilization of meaning (link — 10). The process cannot be put into work by *any* quake — it would crash itself. Then, by meaning of interconnections of all parts of processes, when there is an indication, we predict any problem as well and these problems come (threshold). If we see no problem, it means we are blind to it, or there is no real job being done. Then something changes (2), but we finally come to the possibility to solve the problem of totality of all business only to the end; however, the meaning of it is at the second stage. If we don't know how the business is going to be finished and do not see the end of process at the beginning, it is not worth it to begin. In order to solve the problem, a lot of work is required. There is task and formula at eight. So, if everything is done correctly, all details are clarified, we find the solution. But there is also the common factor of everything, not entering the process. For example, we can consider ecological problem if it is a plant with its production. Or demands of the market. Grants or credits, other things. It's for seventh stage. Then, seven to ten, we return to the beginning, so that it is recurrence.

Diagram of Inactivity

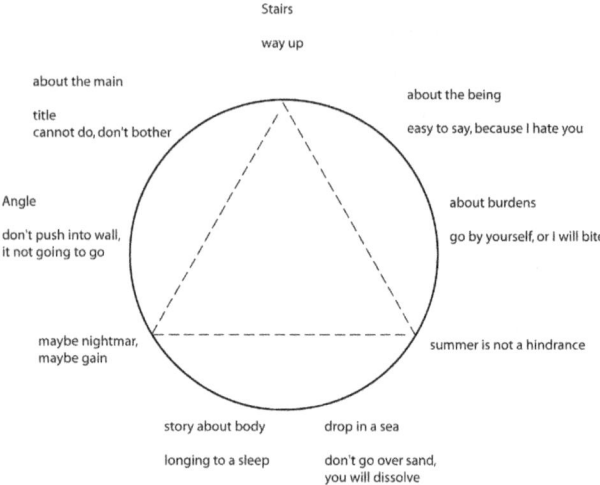

Life demands from us. What is a set of our inactivity? Let us consider different possibilities of it. We think of inactivity in terms of laziness, pressure of the world around us, fear, and all kinds of misacting. What if there are reasons inside oneself? All other reasons are easy to suppose, and this is not an explanation. No one told us that if we have fear, we have to be inactive, or if we have been pressed by someone. By observation we might discover those settings that would bring toward inactivity. In case it's workable, we should be able to enneagram it.

One of the factors, at ten, is actually our desire up, an occupation with this longing. For some reason, it closes something so much that we feel an obligation of not-manifesting. For this reason, there are always different rules, aspiring to manifestation, when something like this goes on to escape this problem. At two, it is also our inadequate reaction in terms of repulsion of certain things, maybe really wrong. We don't want to approach them, and this makes us not do something, even to defend ourselves (for prevention also). At third stage we are overwhelmed by daily activity. We have job, position, necessities. We need to shop, laundry, clean, wash, etc. We became cross to everything seemingly alien to our already present obligations, demands, and occupation. It might be correct but still, we getting overcharged and dislike our way to be crossed. It is different from second stage, where it is about spiritual values and discrimination. Here it is as if we already hold on to something and cannot turn to something else. And yet it is just a daily activity. At four there is a sentence not quite clear. It requires explanations of the term. Hindrance means it is not because of this and summer is the time of vacation. This means it is not for the reason of laziness that we are inactive. And really, our laziness always has some other reason behind it; it is not autonomic. Five, drop in a sea, is when we feel our small position in comparison with someone else; we get humiliated, even willingly, even if it is for the reason not to lose ourselves (dissolution). This way, it is opposition to the second stage when we escape from des-attraction; here it is appreciation but with a conscious desire to escape the action not to put oneself into wrong requirement of playing a role of someone more important than one is, which would lead to pretension. It is also half of the total scheme, corresponding to the tenth position. We also can just be unable to rise and work. As anywhere, at six it is about some negative part. In this way we see that we take different events to put them into one scheme. This gives us the idea of there being different kinds of enneagrams — one that takes the process in its stages and others for appearance. At the seventh stage, it is about our instability in terms of inward apprehension. We do not see position where we are; we are not sure of what action should be taken and if it is required. This is why we are inactive. We can see that our state deteriorated from the beginning further on; it is more passive, but it is more active for the state of inactivity. Things might also be really impossible to be changed (8). Nine, or totality, concerns the action of all kinds of factors. In this way, it might have a title because it is the beginning of the explanation of any situation in its particular case. In its particular terms, it means if one cannot manage it is better not to touch it. It should be conscious if it is inactive, otherwise one would take action even if it is not carried on through in a proper way. Here it is connected with the beginning of the scheme where there is conscious participation.

Enneagram of Lechery and Love in a Sleep

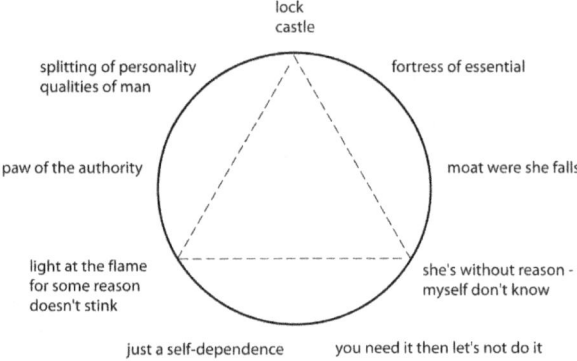

Let's take another example of the diagram with enneagramatic nature on the subject of sex, this time with the theme on concrete subject of inadequacy. We might not wish to do the intercourse in which case we fall into a state of haze and disqualification; it is reassurance. Then we begin to direct our feelings that belong to love and sex into a channel of conceived qualities where it is not manifested outwardly. We discuss here the process of reasons and periodic renewal of these things. Contrary to previous schemes, it is not different reasons of the state, it is situations or incapacities of inadequacy working together. We can use as an example a characteristic person, to use it in abstract. It is as if a conditioned case, to make a show. First, it is a particular self-enclosure inside oneself, for whatever reasons. However, in close observation, if to take an inward octave, it is one and the same case. For the second stage go our inward qualities. It is for what is inside of us. This predisposes necessity of *some* kind of love activity, otherwise there wouldn't be this subject of wrong directory because there would be *no directory*. At three, this stage in a way is downfall because it's the place of entry, so we have to assume there is no entry and line changes or it doesn't require influx. Here it is a pit in which one appears to be fallen. Why? Well, we take a situation where it happens. Taken completely in abstract form, it might be brought to one and the same universal scheme, or it might be using terms for special character of situation. At four, it is phenomenon. It is not one's essence; it is not quite a process of change in character, but it is what makes us believe that there are no reasonable factors behind this or that wish leading to behavior toward *this* goal. This way it might be misinterpreted that there really are no reasons behind it. It might be taken this way as by the very person who doesn't realize one's own wishes so and by the society. Reasons behind it, again, are the same for such cases; it is the misunderstanding of oneself, miss-qualification, weakness of willpower (or interactions), maybe instability, and others.

At five it is particular reaction, but it is predisposed by previous factors. One begins to feel it very strongly, then he is refused in it. In a way, he is already incapable, and this is correct. But there is no correction of the facts of pressure, situational factors, and misgivings; in this way, it leads to the sixth stage, or, one, as a strong-intended person, comes to independence from this necessity through the self-dependence or self-assurance of its permanence. From there one is coming toward possibility to go out of the circumstances or subject them to oneself. Even if one is unable yet, one begins to maintain conscious look on the situation.

At seven, it is the realization of good and bad; we know what the difference is and this is not only about us. Eight is a pressure factor of any social measures from rumor to security or judgment of this or that kind. It is *not* consequences, it is what prevents us.

In a way, ninth and last stage is also the beginning of another sequence. But it also could be viewed as a gathering of all which we used to talk of in this diagram. Its situational nature, however, evolves in a following: we might be approached, once we are out of the situation that used subject us to it prior. We passed through all the stages and now we reach it again. As it is not something disposable, it reaches our end. We don't think of it in terms of social stability only; we cannot go for it just because it is predisposed that there are interactions possible. By the circumstances we are put in the possibility of falling behind the edge, now after cognition of all surrounding. As it is only possibility and we are unstable, we cannot turn to usual ways of immediate safety. We continue turn in the situation in which we find oneself at this moment. In this way, we begin to split our personality. On one side, we keep analyzing, and from another we oppose, but under disguise of everything been as usual as it was. In this way we try to preserve our state from possible intrusions. Paradoxical quality of the scheme consists in the fact that this state of inadequacy, leading to disqualification and blurred mentality, comes from a conscious decision. Almost at every stage there is some opposition, and yet its inactivity leads to wrong channeling of forces where they are locked. The reality of the situation — that it is not our imagination, that there are real reasons, and that we cannot escape — cannot be underestimated.

Let us take an example when all this is completely different. It is willpower and we are led by it. Third stage is impulse one receives by making circumstances impossible, or reacting inadequately. Out of usual way. There is no reason for this, and those who are around also see no reason in it. But for someone, to whom this scheme is applied, it is realization of sudden wish. In this way, it is for one something out of the usual. It might encounter (or lead to) opposition from authority or those who strive to suppress. There is a fortress of essential and it is locked, and there is an outward play of feelings for the continuation of preservation. There is also particular self-control; we cannot follow our every wish or it just might lose its qualities. And we have qualification for discrimination of qualities. And in a way it is self-dependence, otherwise one looks somewhere else in all these situations for the basis to have a back up. This transformation of the situation discussed beforehand is predisposed by the fact it is conscious, and by the character in general.

Enneagram of Energy and Loss

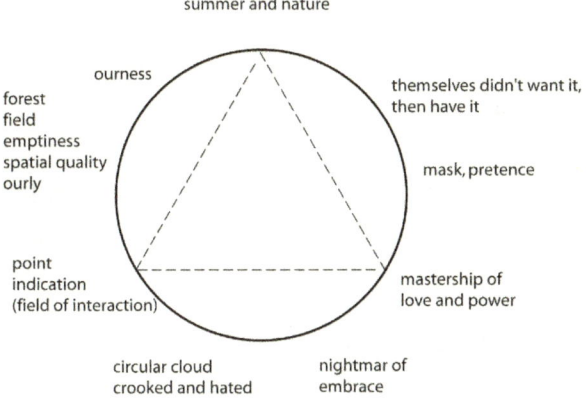

This is enneagram of energy and loss. It includes different factors for fulfillment of totality. At ten it is the basis of natural appraisal which is governing fluidity of process. It is connected with stage seven, carrying the indicative factor of directory and spatial dimensions. At four, another basis of triad of will, there is a natural quality of energy. Other stages experience different transactions inside and out of what subject is under hand, and there could be different applications of this schematic plan. Stage six, a negative transaction, is very important. Our energy could be directed toward enclosure or limited disabilities to preserve the fact of inability. In this case, powers are lost; they've been spent on preservation of connected, circular movement without possibility to act. It is negation and brings all kinds of pathology. There is also atmosphere around such a factor; because its exit cannot be controlled, all control goes to feed energy circulation. Point nine has a strange name. Really, there is something undefined in all energetic manifestations, which we also feel as personally belonging to us. Point three is always demonstrative; it is a shell, which might be refilled or emptied. This invariably comes with stage six, and it is an active part of a different kind of nature, not opposing but relating more to function. This triad relates to the *loss* of energy. Stage five is a personification. We do not know, but we feel it. Then, it leads to psychosis. In the second stage, situation gets invariably connected with downward pour of energetic transaction. We might understand what is going on but cannot stop the process. This triad 8-5-2 has in it in particular a presence of our noticing. It is sensual. The eighth stage is for us noticing, but while we flow into what surrounds us. We accept the fact that if something vaporizes, it is of our preference; there is a natural feeling of belonging, that we *belong* to the spatial unreality and nature.

Experiential Enneagrams

Let us introduce another kind of enneagramatic participation of connected features, or nine stages connected into one slice of reality. There are automatic reactions, which lead to one kind of action upon a leveled field, not limited (or limited), but just upon one level of these qualities of experience. For this reason, they could be called experiential. But there are completely different qualities in us, and what we are capable of would answer this or that stage of them. It means, what is for one of us a table, for another is a party with noise and drink and food.

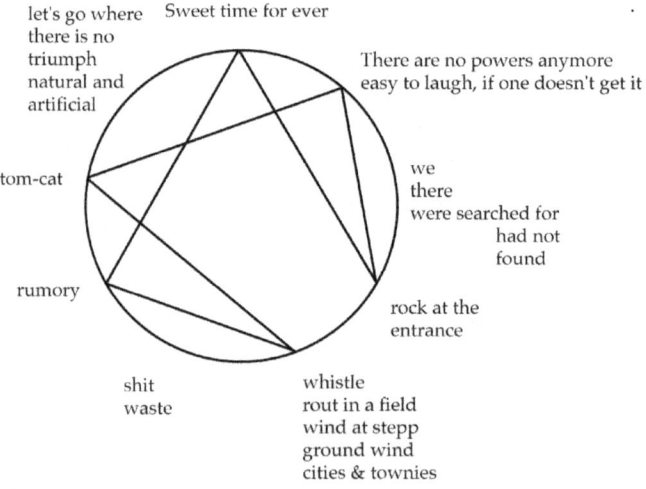

Story of Enneagram

All stages answer certain qualities in us of experience. There is reaction (4), activity (3), mental values (5), wish factor (9), other. Chemistry might give us even a complete arrangement of all substances, present at these states, with variations for each special case. Let us take an example where it is not an empty scheme of reactions, but it is filled by someone's developed individuality. We can be flat or superficial. We also can get very sophisticated. It would also have a mark on our experience. In this way, we also talk of our being. So, the experiential enneagrams are for our reaction on existence.

This scheme period could be viewed in a way of process of existence, sequence:

10	it is inward feeling of capacity, particular for me
2	result of meeting of us and the world
3	I cannot be found
4	some problem, here it is a hindrance before entry (or after)
5	recognition of requirement to go
6	presence of what isn't important
7	noise around the fact
8	inward concentration for preservation
9	loss and incapacity

Period is clearly defined, as out of my state I move to the problem, after the entrance into somewhere, so I experience the hindrance. Then, it is, in *this* case, exhaust from all of the work being done, and one can laugh over my efforts but I won't. After this, as there is absence of powers, man moves into preservation; it is a natural quality of a particular character. This character is not only flirting, it is its general behavior so that one acquires the possibility to escape and be functional. There is always a waste, but, in actuality, there are necessities, and someone recalls not so important things. After it we have a recollection that we need return to work, or we are demanded somewhere. We are on the road, and need to go. This brings a feeling of freedom. Actions bring to rumor. These are consequences and we are already gone (9) and come back to our initial state. As everywhere, ten is *more* than other stages because it is on the order higher.

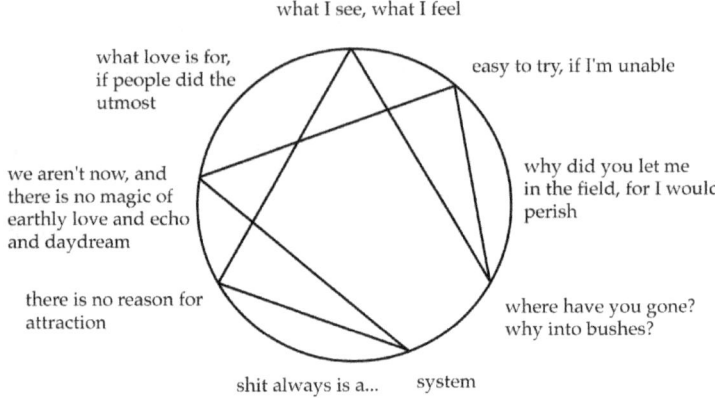

Let us take an example of another person. He would have quite other experience. His experience of perception is what I see, what I feel (10). Then it is the inability with special character; it is that one is ready or willing to be able to accomplish, only it for some reason would not work with the feature that it is easy to try. Either there are absent some features necessary for reaching, but yes, it is like working in one room where there are no materials for production, and this is easy because there are no real efforts afterward, no tension in trial, even though there is a wish to. Then it is weakness toward the world. One cannot survive and yet he was put on his own so he complains. At four it is of a slippery quality of things escaping. System — it means, for one person, at this case, it is putting everything into some kind of value list with exemplifications and explanations so that it is explained, like this. Six is for a personal attitude toward what one hates, but it is also an indication that one is troubled by it. At point seven, if it won't be filled with personal identity toward everything, it is no attraction. In our experience we not always are attracted. We are looking for attraction all the time. But mostly out of the state of not being attracted at the moment. Here, in this scheme, it is that *there is no reason* for attraction, whatever it means. At eight, without any personal feature, it is absence; here this absence has that tint that we feel what we love is not present if we are made to be absent. The last stage is an explanation of process character, as it is a totality of phenomena (9). It should hold all qualities. For this scheme of someone's experience, it is that one believes it to be impossible to apply to what he would like to, if he feels the situation to be polluted.

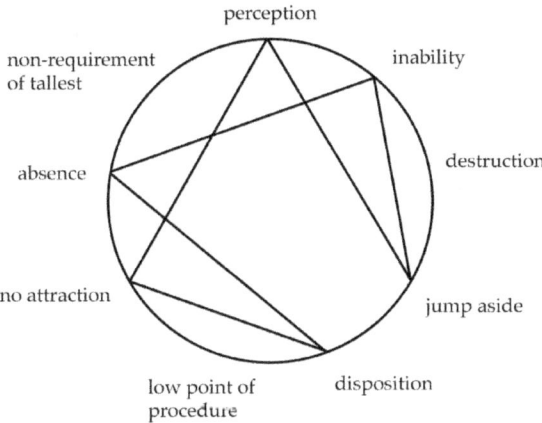

Full Experiential Enneagram.

If it is filled, then it acquires qualities of meaning, connected for us with associations.

Here there is empty experiential enneagram for this subject. It really works the way it is with people who do not have anything except their personality. In a way, there is almost no personal qualities entering into experience. This way, scheme is almost clear and could be introduced on its own. Once a man had a perception of something, he doesn't go into it, but jumps aside. It is an inability, one is incapable to control oneself in the situation where something touches his feelings . Out of it there is absence. It is funny to say, but after this situation when he's incapable, there is nothing possible except this absent. Then, it is disposition. Having nothing to do, as there is none for the one because there was *none* and nothing was accepted from without, this whoever has to decide what to do and what it is about. So, he thinks. This supposition has nothing to do with the situation; it is self-preservation to be and farther on like this. But, as there is a lot of basic things in life, one just forgets and gets involved in it, as there are no other things to occupy with, and what is his reaction is that he has *no attraction*. Then he again perceives, as he wasn't attracted to anything, therefore he needs to look to the outside again and the process is repeating. So, it's a complete waste.

Intermission

Salt and sugar
Salt never is a story, it is a beginning. Salt is cold. Salt is to the point.

Enneagram of Sugar; Modal

Let us take not symbolic but modal enn of sugar. This means we can apply anything toward the scheme that would correspond to the same setting of factors. Or this is already *not* about sugar. We can tell that sugar in what it is corresponds to some scheme, which we try to revive. By the qualities, story could be initiated. Its passive part of function is that it is dissolvable. As subjected to action, it is picked up. We never pick up salt, we spread it. As it is often in story tales, we mark the way with it; it is white, but if to mark with sugar, it might be pulled away by ants, as it is sweet. No one would spread sugar because it is of a spoiling nature, would mark the cloth, stick, and make it sticky. As its initial state, it is out of clear pressure; it is soft and has no outlook. It is not ironic, not critical, it is a rumor. Sugar also has qualities of warmth and freshness. This has drawback as it is cannot be used too often. We might tell it's egoistic. To need a cup of tea, we pick it up, as it has a dissolvable nature, and dissolve it in warm water; we continue.

Story of Enneagram

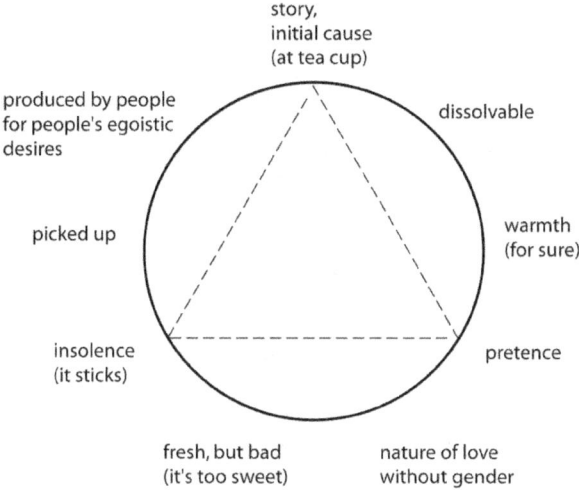

Enneagram of an Apple

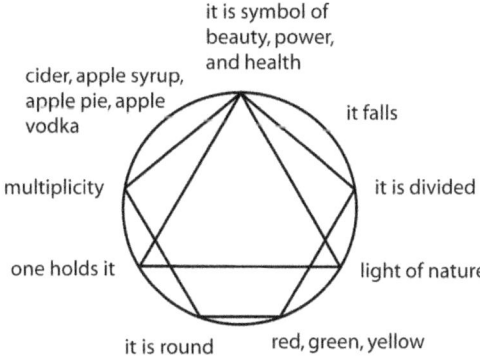

This is an example of enneagram with mixed identifications of the same subject. Some descriptions relate to symbolic, and other to physical characteristics. In a way it is legal because when we think of an apple it is already connected for us with a set of associations; this is why it happened this way, not just a subject or just an abstract idea. At six, the crucial point, it is said that it is round. In fact, it means that it is roll-able. As long as it rolls there is a change. It's a choice. It been used by Greeks in mythology, where an apple was given to one of the three goddesses who claimed to be the most beautiful.

Theory of Lechery

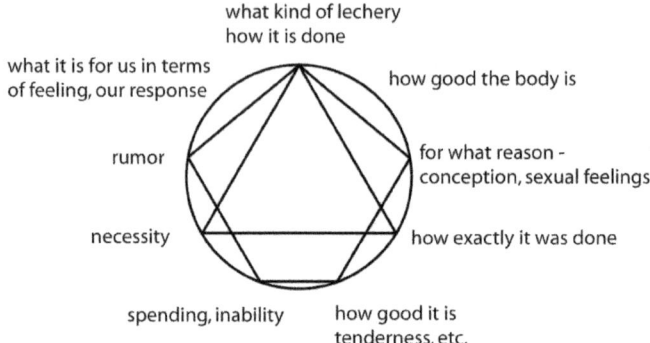

Here is the phenomenal enn of *lechery*. Let's review the stages, how they go. At ten enters classification in general, as it is on the order higher. So, in this case it is what kind of lechery and how this is happening or being done. Our physiological state means a lot. Here it is at number two. When we are healthy, strong, even beautiful, it is one thing, and another when these qualities aren't present.

Section Four

Theorem of Non-Opposition to the High

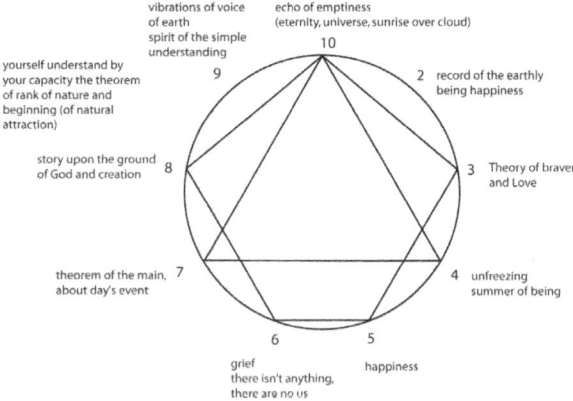

By this diagram we express the supposition that there is a preexistent requirement not to oppose to something high.

There are reasons for our non-opposition to what is demanded from above, and these are predisposed. Subject is taken from eternity, reason of existence (ten). What we have upon the diagram, another set of writing in between the eighth and ninth stations, is an entry of shock at the place of interval.

As long as there is no us, no one who we are attracted to, there is no meaning, therefore, and it is grief. Its opposition is happiness. It is connected then with the theory of bravery and love, or what *we* are attracted to. Our existentiality (4). And why it is important (7). We are doing something this way, because before we used to confront something with such and such issues and results. This way, we collect the memory, or recollection of how it used to be, and our attitude to it.

It is stage second. And we feel good, so we are not against it. But then, there are higher parts; they fall upon eighth and ninth steps, if nine is like shamanic realization, eight is the developed capability of religious studies or cosmogony. The entry of shock in between is our personal capability of understanding this theory and natural attraction.

Theory of Bravery and Love (Friendship)

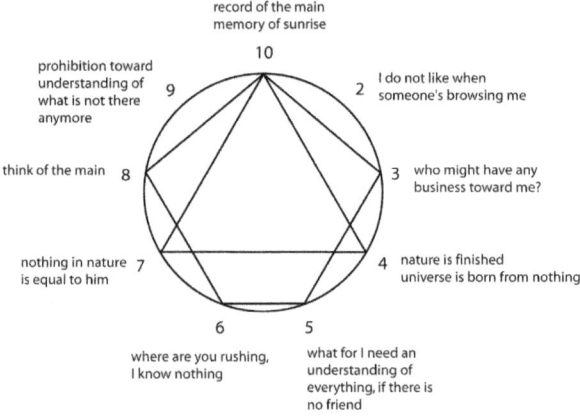

Knowledge of there being attraction doesn't yet explain the feature of how it is correct, if it is, why it is sometimes wrong, and what it is about. There is no comparison in this scheme; it speaks about the feature, even though there is entry, but it is impossible not to have because if we have the ability to love, we might hate as an opposition and distraction. What is not there is the explanation why. This means all this is based upon something; this is a theory, for me, because there is not necessarily the same reaction for everyone. Anyway, this scheme presupposes that one has an attitude, likeability to one, and repulsive reaction toward another.

One of the easier stages to understand is the fifth and also the seventh (consider arrows). It is our requirement to share or even just the need of communication, socializing, and exchange, or we can need no aim. We do not need to understand then, and this is what belongs to the common scheme (preceding enneagram). The seventh is the iden-

Story of Enneagram

tity of the beloved; we consider it almost artificial (octaves). Comparing with it the fourth station, it has 'nature is finished.' If the universe is born from nothing, where did the universe come from? This stage is for phenomena, so in *this* case it is the end for phenomena and nature of the universe's arousal is unknown. Our repulsion toward unnecessary interruption is expressed at the third stage, with idea of belonging to something else, which one might consider important. From this side, it is improper to approach, but in its nature, it is a passive force because we have no recognition of the act of opposition. Stage six is contrary to a critical approach of the futuristic kind, as the aim, or target, lies ahead of someone's rush. It is the necessary feeling which one has, unless we don't participate completely, which is impossible for this subject of recognition. This way, it is a theory, because we know nothing of the other's aim. The ninth stage is a passive one for us, as we are under pressure. The meaning of the slogan is it is already gone, as it was prohibited, and now we have no access, no desire, to reach it. And we never have an understanding of this prohibition really taking place, and we now lose contact with it. Still, we always have the memory of what has happened, with feelings toward it (ten) and thought in general terms (eight). The second is survival; we have no reason to desire anyone taking considerations on our state or destination.

Theorem of the Main

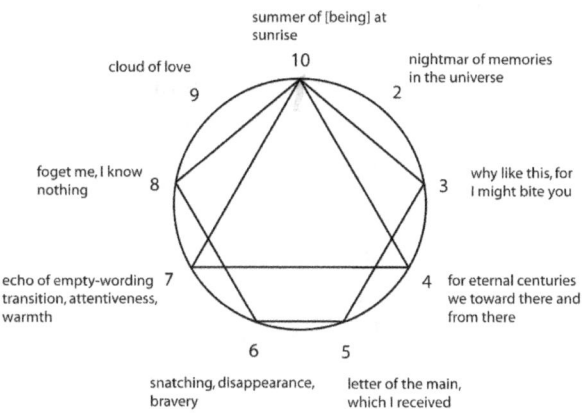

Theorem—a form which does not have a logical explanation, but whose true employment is clear. Its prerequisites are that it should work a particular amount of directions toward the future; if the setting changes its four dimensions, it won't work. Heretofore, this scheme, as theorem of main, is for something indispensable for us in our setting of how our world is. This is the meaning of it being the theorem of the main.

When we see the placement of meaning for the theme, at staging, we touch upon the ground of the individual in a universal scheme, where it is predisposed, yet it is not necessarily required. What is interesting here is that it is still a theorem—that is, it is the only way *this* works. In this way it is higher than the theory of love because it cannot even be touched otherwise and it cannot be taken in different terms. The stages, as follows, should obviously correspond to connection and interactivity; there the scheme and clear outline might be possible. When we think of what makes up our day, we often consider the whole, how was it? When we agree that the day was okay, we feel it as predisposed; this is why another name is 'of the day's event.' The tenth stage is exemplification of calamity. It is something as if used to be before. Second is for the feeling of drowning in something we don't understand. We have no access to realize what surrounds us. It is all up and down. At three it is a temper. We know what might be permissible to be done to us. It is not necessary an aim (because we have attitude), or is clearly manifested. Fourth stage is a striving toward the horizon. But we had to start from somewhere. This might be now at the horizon behind us. So we move and run out of somewhere. The reaction of it, of interactivity in between fourth and second stages, is of active opposition, and this is natural. Fifth stage is for the influx of the information. Sixth stage is for us to be daring to go, as life requires bravery. Its another side is, meaning disappears when we try to catch it. Then it is seventh stage. It has few slogans. We know it is not done and we suffocate in the world of polluted flower. Words are done, and it is wrong to know. We are on the way, and maybe everything would exchange. It is in transition. Time is running. We change, remain the same. We pay attention. There is warmth. It is conglomeration of power, to go on. Eighth stage is for absence of desire and understanding, at this moment. Desire to subside for the world. Nine is for the cloud of love, in the atmosphere. It is external, on its own.

The Descending Enneagram on the Theme of Transgression

Going down, sliding

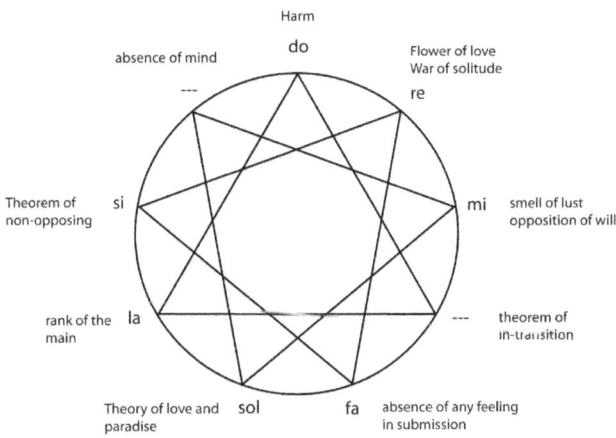

Harm, because any transgression involves it.
Rank of the main—that is, scale of values.
Interval—here there is an entry. If there won't be an entry, there would be no harm. It is eight stage, so we go down, from ten. As it is descending enneagram. This way we encounter this interval. So, at this place, a possibility of harm is coming, and then it is initiated. Otherwise there would be another enneagram.
If there won't be a scale of values, harm won't be able to be estimated. We know harm is done because something precious was spoiled.

Higher interval: we are incapable of controlling a situation and of transcribing it, but as we have a knowledge of what is happiness (sol,) our will would oppose what is destructible for this better side. So, *mi* is the reconciling force in between what is at the other corners of the triangle — sol mi.

Si-fa-re: The real feelings in us — the desire to have a love and be loved. Submission without any feeling and non-opposition. In this way there is permission from one side to be harmed. So, it's a sliding enneagram to the factor of non-opposition.

If we would be able to control the situation, there would be no harm; it would be another enneagram. *Do* is at the top, but it doesn't begin from harm, it is the result, the *do*, or consequences. The whole descending octave is set after the interval because the recipient has no control over the situation. In this way, tenth stage is ever-present possibility of here being a harm. So, we could've get into this situation.

Enneagram of Reflection of Love into Nature of Conscience and Echo of Perception

We might have in oneself a particular constitution of matter, or elements, of fine substance, and this would produce a reaction in people around — our immediate ones, far ones, farther upon the distance. We walk the street and it is okay for us, but one might

suppose it is the requirement of continuation; and he stops us, deciding, this is a right trait to show his compassion and interest. There is a lot of predisposed ones; we might do the same. The fact is it is almost not us. We know we do not need it. We know we play the fool. What is the wrong thing? Everything one does is a mechanism of predisposition. There presupposed to be a scheme, which we traverse. We can use this scheme willingly. Then when we need, we might stop, realizing what we are doing. Then there are no wrong consequences for us and others. What we need to do is get out from where it happens. We can view oneself ascending step by step. These stages being as if put for us, from top to the down. This is nature of descending enneagram, it goes both ways simultaneously. It is a clockwise movement when we are going by our perception, contrary-clockwise. This way, the position of the stages are in continuation, but for us it is an immediate experience maybe connected in terms of its identification and increase of subject, but a momentum is the definition of experience. As it is descending enneagram, we take it as it is usually presented, with points from one to nine, with nine at the upper corner of central triangle. The meaning of this stage is, there is nothing in one that would correspond to whatever subject someone else might have. As long as it is not where one really is, another person cannot decide or solve it. All this is totality of process, or phenomenon. This way, every stage belongs simultaneously for the process and one's experience. This is traditional enneagram. However, upon the scheme I'm using three triangles. This is a homage to Raimond Lulli, a thirteenth century mystic, who used such symbol in his works. But it of course has a period 1-4-2-8-5-7. This process, if we begin from one, starts from there as one not being in decisive position. There is nothing concentrated in one. But it isn't blindfolding, there is expectation. This way it begins. So, stage is set up. But, my attitude is, why anyone would play around there in the field. Then, at two, we have the insinuation of pressure; as the recipient, one cannot count upon other people's judgment but they also don't really need it, so it is mechanicality. But, put willingly by law, they cannot continue without pressure. Why were they ever interested in us? Nothing might help, as it is just the right move done, and no need to correct it. Then it is separation, point five. Here it doesn't play that role, as when it is a pentagram as we have no ten. Five, creative point, put upon a stage—we know, but they continue? Whatever. Where is the rumor from? I don't understand, I mean it, because as with this pressure, I could just be gone. I do not know. So, are they not happy with proceeding? All this is definitely from leisure time; *they* are not occupied. They have time to occupy by talk and judgment and resolution, spread for all. I might be bitter, but it means nothing. No considerations. Then I can't and I just cannot have it. So, what is the solution-for. Such is the circle. Then, for a periodic one, from one to four, meaning of the line it is an action not corresponding to someone's understanding. From four to second, it is someone's reaction upon it, two to eight — the predicament of loss or incapability. Eight to five is a suppression of feelings. We also turn our look upon the world. Five to seven – we have our reaction. And they have a celebration. The meaning of a line from seven to one is not a return at the beginning, it is the realization of who they are, and their actual terms with the world (nine). We need it.

Theorem of Restoration of Natural Qualities [Of *Her* Essence]

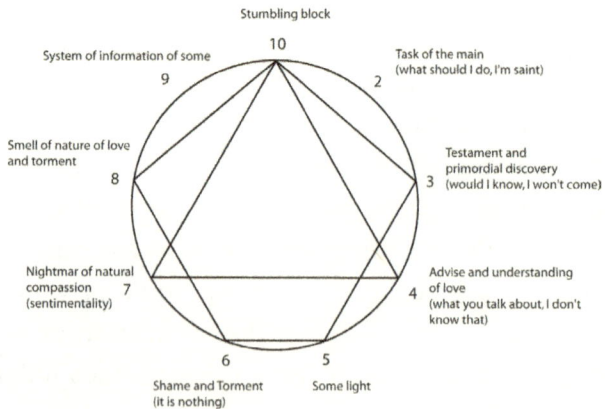

These are two enns on restoration of natural qualities for *him* and *her*. The stages are inter-swap, so they can be considered together, but the flow is different and so are the results. For her it is a preference, for him also, and these preferences are different. His outlook is out of egoistic desires, hers is more striving toward reality, the consequences outlook, and a search for natural qualities of fulfillment. The opposition in between of male and female lasts for a long term. There are tendencies of what woman is looking for and what a man might follow. We don't have to blame one of them. All the stages are put in accordance, but as a flow of process. One can make a treasure or trash out of it, but this not required by the schematic output. What one can consider is coming out of it with the result of inclusion of the former, past experience into the row of similar consequences of proceeding one's life. Certain things could be predicted. This is example of one of them. Further issues could be taken out, as if it did not happen. Man is destroyed, as there won't be restoration of self. It is good for us that we don't decide such things, should we make a restoration of self or should we get destroyed. If the restoration happens, this is how it is. We also can pose a question, if it would be the same process when the restoration is required, and the answer is yes. And is it inescapably the fall of man if there is no restoration, and the answer is no. This way, we see a special process behind which might lead to the destruction of self, or un-participation and escape, and this is not necessary for *any* interaction between humans.

Juliette Eden

Theorem of Restoration of Natural Qualities [Of *His* Essence]

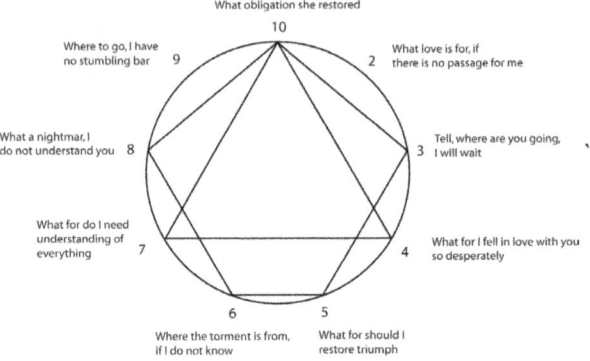

The White Color

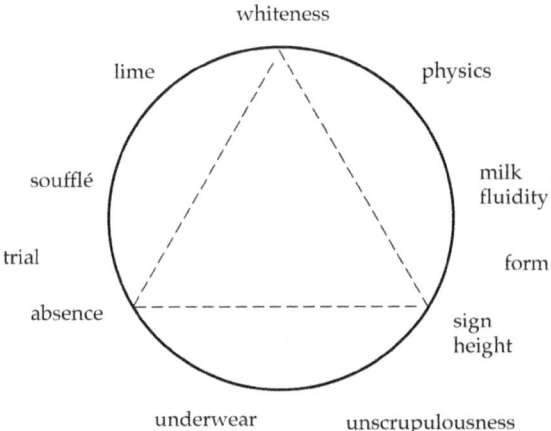

Form (one casts into it)

Trial (rough sheet of paper)

3 – reflection about the future   milk, fluidity

8 – relation about the future   soufflé

This is synthesis.

As in the enneagram of lechery and love in a sleep, if to take it as an example of also a modal enn, lock and castle there (10) is for the structure, meaning it is physical. 2 is fortress of essential and is therefore content. Here it is physics. White is something we can see outside of when we observe. Therefore, physics here — we don't have to forget that each time it is for the inner quality of *this* color, different for every other color then, not just a physical. 3 of the before mentioned enn, moat where she falls, is now the fall and the invariable structure *around* the castle. This way, these three stages go together to function in its materiality, even though it might seem an abstract question. Four, she's without a reason, speaks about our personal requirements for which no one might find an explanation. This way it is as well a visual demonstration as a castle. Fifth, 'you need, then let's not do it,' means refusal. Sixth is just a self-dependence; it is the manifestation and activity of willpower. This way, these three stages are for the inward qualities. 7 is light at the flame for some reason does not stink — that is, again there is no reason. Paw of the authority is a negative factor for triangle 2-5-8, because if there is essence (2) and refusal, then why would it come? Here is an explanation of where it comes from. The splitting of personalities happens because she falls and there is a will, so this is how it works. Here, in this scheme, milk, fluidity, is now a manifestation of the factor in the physical realm. To understand what form means, we need to discuss further stages. Sign and height is a signature of the factor. It is far and all white. Five and six. Underwear is something that no one sees but us, and maybe close friends, but it does exist. Absence—this way, we close the central triangle. Here is the form, if it is fluidity; it invariably assumes that it might flow into form. When it is absence, we can try and soufflé is now a result; it is mixture. Lime is an element. It has a physical existence in terms of being a set of waves of particular length. This set would differ for each of the colors. Downward there is a trial to produce the same scheme for some of the other colors.

Transparent	Blue	Green
10 transparency	of blue	of green
2 physics	- -	- -
3 wireless	sky	growth, link, transforming
-- wire	breath	vitality
4 trace	heaven	system of preservation
5 transcendence	depth, dome	existence
6 atmosphere	penetration	development
7 no way	air	nature
-- stepping stones	to hold movement	fall
8 crystal	concentration	swamp
9 alcohol	ozone	hydrogen

Here is transparency and its natural qualities of the physical. Its nature is wireless. Trace means it is invariably wire as its physical object, if it is possible to produce. Five and six — everyone can see it, it is not hidden. No way — one doesn't go into the wall. This way, it is open. But, it is as a glass wall, there is no way. This way, there is no way, and it is stepping stones. As in preceding scheme, where there is an absence and we try. And we receive a crystal — it is structure. Alcohol — a quality manifested itself in the physical world.

When we speak of blue, we get in touch with another realm of factors. We can feel it as a strange power in the world, maybe we never understood it. We took no opinion of it. Now we can. Of blue — it is akin of it being white. It is sky, and therefore it's breath. It is a positive factor of agreement, not opposition (as in between 7 and 8). Heaven. This way, we can see the connection in between four and five. Trace and transcendence — we can make far going issues. As long as it is heaven. It is a dome. Is it a depth, or its exemplification? Atmosphere envelops, it is around, here it is penetration. Air and its opposition — we hold our breath. Concentration. Ozone.

Story of Enneagram

When we talk of modal enneagrams, it is complicated in terms of we do not know the subject. When it is about colors, we can tell or see them as having qualities of numbers, as I put it down in my first book, self-published as *Enneagram in Color*. Here, it would be white for the ten, blue for eight, green for seven, yellow for six, light-coffee for five, lavender for the four; for three it is red, and grey for two. It is akin to the level of stratums into which we can reappear. Nine is orange. It is not a symbolism of colors, as we talk of model.

Common Enneagram

This is a common enneagram, combining the structure of production (period of functional trans-activity), a pentagram, and an inward triangle in a circle. The only step, not entering into any of the figures, is marked with a small circle on the circumference. This way, we should've see there both existential and functional processes. For this reason is taken the example on the theme of our aspiration and move of activity so that there are different natures around, combined. As it is a functional process, the periodic line is seen upon the scheme, meaning trans-activity. We go from up to ten, from ten to four, etc. This way, let's discuss the first step as step seven, prior the move from it to the highest point of pentagram. This stage enters into period, and also is a corner at the base of the triangle, making a frame of the process. It corresponds to the law of octaves (seven) in its nature of activity of requirement of adding the force at the interval, which is going to be at step eight before 'entering' the whole — ninth. This stage, initially, is one of the three powers, making up a visual world, a world of abstract ideas, etc. Stages eight and three are supposed to come up from the connection of it with the source, executed at ten. This way, the octave makes up for the intervals. Here we are, with everything, relating to the stage.

For the process in discussion of our aspiration and power, we need to know the problems. These problems arise out of our misconception as well as real factors. For our reaction it matters not, is there a real cause from which torture comes, or it is our reaction upon factors not really supposing to evoke it, but hurting us for the reason they are connected for us by association with a conflicting circumstances. People spend a lot of time trying to organize the factors of their misbehavior. We speak of real facts of continuation. This way, stage seven, the fruit of the process, is our reaching the goal, product of our inspiration, and aim. It means we are in full power (see Enneagram of Light (Universal Enneagram at the beginning). Does someone else loves or hates our idol, for us means nothing. We continue to work toward it, with or without considerations.

This way, the entry of octave is for the *meaning* of content; what exactly is it that makes up our mind and spirit. Point nine is discussed later. This way, the intentional line seven-ten of actual process is from the production of our inspiration to what is called at the stage of the theorem of knowledge of everything. As any theorem, contrary from theory, it supposes to be one and the same, without proof, as it is the one of knowledge of everything; we suppose there is the possibility of knowledge of this or that having reflection in the eternal world of possible info. This way, our inspiration and move of activity are coming from the base of all knowledge, as it is the source, (or at least shown on the diagram). The meaning of the line in connection is we reach or try to reach the possible source, even in its detailed view.

Down by the line ten-four of the initial force to the change, legality, law of four, as phenomenal existence, we have here therefore some kind of continuation of the process. Here it is actually whatever is making up the content, any treasure impression, etc., and the outcome. The meaning of the line is, therefore, transubstantiation, or exemplification, recognition of what we think there should be in the world, seeing and experiencing it now in the phenomenal realm. Third stage appears from connection of source with rule of octave (10 and 7) by means of deduction. (10-7-3) Three is a triplicity of things. As the right part of the diagram belongs to existence, as a factor of triadic power, and a place of interval, if we have the knowledge, but don't reach the aim, we have revulsion. In terms of the triadic nature, it is us, our consideration in comparison with what there should be, some ideal, and understanding. The four elements of the fourth stage are reflection, what makes a reflection, our experience and intention, our goal, and what we are looking for. The entry at the interval is, though undefined, an understanding. It is not clear why we would accept anything after revulsion. Or how we are feeling after the lack of powers about our aim and wish, how can we still hope and occupy with it. It is if we come sequentially to stage four after three over the circumference. We, therefore, think of it as a place of entry of something, which would acknowledge our aim of interplay and gambling.

At the base of pentagram, the fifth stage is composed of a primary source and law of four so that our knowledge and experience makes us wish for it to be longer. We understand we are not going to be there forever. Sixth stage is transition, and also the darkening of reason. In this scheme, it means we just think and feel, in this way it is calamity, and yet a transition out of this state. Returning to the period, these two points of pentagram, appearing from connection of the source with two initial forces, five and eight, are connected by the line. We can substitute anything toward it, but its meaning is there is no aim, and, therefore, it is aggressiveness (five-seven) because we do not care.

Another line of four-two of the periodic transaction is to touch the situational factor. We are in the situation through our experience, and have a revulsion. Being born as humans, we need to survive. Yet we have aims, purposes, etc. We challenge. We might not be able, but we feel it. In transactions as well. We get lecherous while bearing this. And are tormented by the pull we feel. This way, line two-eight is for possible resolution, finding an application. A partly hypnotization is for line four-two. So, we could exist. Opposite of the second stage is a reaction of belonging also to the negative triad of the nine-fold structure, and it is its active force. We might not be able to acknowledge anything at all; this way we refuse for whoever it is his natural law of development or evolution. We can perceive it as a positive factor, definitely as giving as power, need to go, see, or discriminate, contrary from the second stage on the move down.

If we would look for the common scheme in the middle of the book, then three fastenings in between the periodic lines are: fastening of the beginning, in between ten-four and two-eight, our coming to existentiality and search or coming for the content. Then the task of the main, of crossing of two-eight and seven-ten, or reaching the aim. And, eight-five, no aim, with seven-ten, or reaching it, is longing to work.

AFTER-WORD

There is pentagramatic existence, as a law of five general components. These are fixed or put amid other positions, playing their definite parts. Indefinite row of other situations is unpredictable. We might view any process in its six components, or five, that would be just a pentagram without other poses. As long as we put pentagram into a set of nine components, with connections in them, it is a difficult, intricate pattern, they don't go along in a simple way. Talking of pentagram, invariably we need to have ten at the upper angle of central triad because five is half of ten; therefore, there is a correspondence in between them. All kinds of manipulations could be produced, but it won't give us understanding of the nature of the processes. Or events, of phenomenal nature, we still know nothing. Just some entry into psychology and physiology as well applied to the scheme, does not explain yet why the process might be discovered through the perspective of it having nine parts. It might just be the ability to see through this complicated figure some of the supposition. Not really any subject was truly appreciated in its full, and this is impossible. A lot of objections are left aside, and considerations. Someone might have tendency to view everything in a stiffened way. I don't think it is required, and do not want that to be important for me if it would continue to be that way. We can take this or that subject to observe it, but we should not do it, if we not become involved. One can discover other things behind the text of each enneagram. We tend to see in other's creations what never was intended to be there by those who've done it. But, we think we are correct. We also tend to underestimate. One does not have to consider me as the source of what is proceeding. I'm only who I am. We never know if words do make sense or don't, especially with such a subject as I reviewed, which cannot be checked and seen. In a way, the process of writing was providing me with a possibility of good artistry of form, but I do not want to show this as the only matter of subject, really. If there is anything artistic, behind this creativity there is only the intention to do this as long as one can and to be able to continue. The form was chosen so as to provide the reader with better intention to participate in appreciation of text and not slip over. Some predisposition, as the possibility of the reader not to read in sequence, also was taken in, as it was how I was writing. Some are sequential. One should wonder why at all such a book was written, and I have no explanation, but a lot of books come out and this is just one of them.

Answer to Nonexistential Enneagram (page)

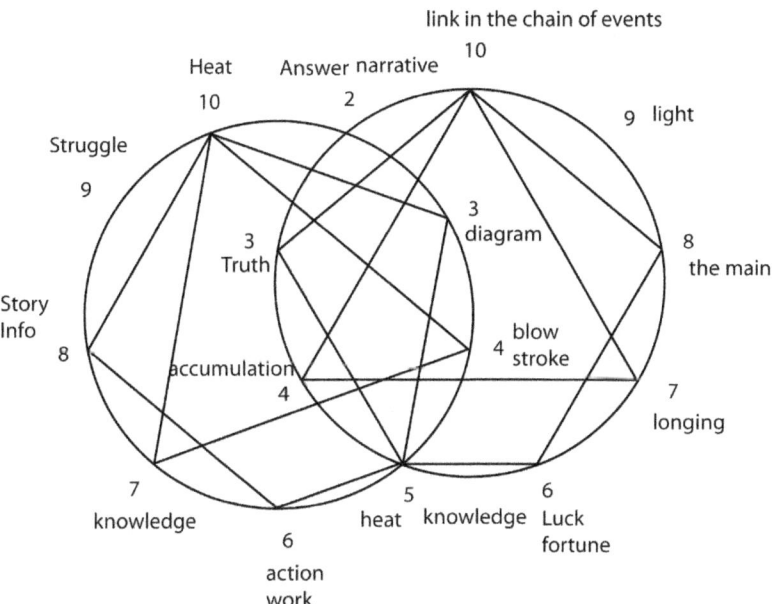

It is a computer. It has a data, and it gives answer if it's questioned.

www.ingramcontent.com/pod-product-compliance
Lightning Source LLC
Chambersburg PA
CBHW031150020426
42333CB00013B/593